Gifts
Handed
Down

Gifts
Handed
Down

J. Daniel Hess

HERALD PRESS
Scottdale, Pennsylvania
Waterloo, Ontario

Library of Congress Cataloging-in-Publication Data
Hess, J. Daniel (John Daniel), 1937-
    Gifts handed down / J. Daniel Hess.
        p. cm.
    Includes bibliographical references.
    ISBN 0-8361-9047-5 (alk. paper)
    1. Virtues. 2. Christian life. 3. Conduct of life. 4. Hess, J.
Daniel (John Daniel), 1937- . I. Title.
BV4630.H47 1996
241'.4—dc20   96-1415
                                                           CIP

The paper used in this publication is recycled and meets the minimum requirements of American National Standard for Information Sciences—Permanence of Paper for Printed Library Materials,
ANSI Z39.48-1984.

An earlier version of "Civility" appeared in *The Marketplace* (May-
June 1995). "Integrity" is a revision of chapter 1 in *Integrity: Let Your
Yea Be Yea* (Herald Press, 1978); a version of the same chapter was
also published in *The Marketplace* (Jan.-Feb. 1996). Scripture is used
by permission, all rights reserved, and unless otherwise indicated
is from the *New Revised Standard Version Bible,* copyright 1989, by
the Division of Christian Education of the National Council of the
Churches of Christ in the USA. KJV, from *King James Version of The
Holy Bible.* NEB, from *The New English Bible,* © The Delegates of the
Oxford University Press and the Syndics of the Cambridge
University Press, 1961, 1970.

GIFTS HANDED DOWN
Copyright © 1996 by Herald Press, Scottdale, Pa. 15683
        Published simultaneously in Canada by Herald Press,
        Waterloo, Ont. N2L 6H7. All rights reserved
Library of Congress Catalog Number: 96-1415
International Standard Book Number: 0-8361-9047-5
Printed in the United States of America
Cover art and book design by Gwen M. Stamm

05 04 03 02 01 00 99 98 97 96 10 9 8 7 6 5 4 3 2 1

To Mervin M. Hess
(1913-1994)

Daddy, you

- took pride in a straight furrow
- talked to the cows
- refused to water the steers on the morning they
  went to the yards
- preferred to work the fields rather than sell
  produce on the streets
- took charge of a work crew, not by word or
  command, but by getting to work
- mowed your own fencerows and then continued
  on to do the neighbors'
- valued a photograph showing the north field
  of potatoes in full bloom
- befriended the German prisoners who helped
  to harvest potatoes
- distinguished between Herr, Stehman, and
  Utz potato chips
- left farmwork behind to help set up the Lancaster
  Conference tent

- seldom drank tea or coffee
- objected strongly to war
- thought Harry Truman used bad words
- never uttered a racial slur
- stayed home occasionally from Sunday night
  church to play ball in the yard

- didn't use alcohol except to put a whiskey-soaked bandage on a chain-saw wound
- made no audible judgments but considered Mt. Gretna, Long's Park, Hershey, and the shore to be worldly locations
- preferred Chevies to Fords, Farmalls to John Deeres, and de Laval to Surge milkers
- smoked a cigar one time because the doctor told you to blow warm smoke into a child's infected ear
- almost cried, when you were seventy, as you told about your accidental shooting of your dog when you were twelve

- sang high tenor for "On the Jericho Road" with Lester Charles, Arthur Miller, and Hiram Strickler Jr.
- read the Bible, the *Intel*, the Sunday school quarterly, and *Farm Journal*
- enjoyed listening to sermons by Sanford Shetler, Harold Eshlemen, and Elias Kulp
- helped to start a youth group at church
- paid tuition to send your children to Mennonite schools
- visited your Sunday school class members
- climbed the highest rafters at a barn raising
- cooked potatoes, string beans, and ham
- grunted in disapproval after reading Drew Pearson in the *Intel*
- seldom if ever told a joke
- shied away from highfalutin people
- had no stomach for high stress
- praised your mother's fried potatoes

- stood an erect six-feet tall
- never voted

- did not give gifts and seldom gave compliments; your charity was anonymous
- embraced your grandchildren with deep affection
- commented favorably on people who kept their shoulders back
- didn't swim, jog, or exercise, but lifted feed bags
- scoffed at health fanatics who ate lettuce sandwiches
- suspected that formal education, high-career jobs, and even church work caused some people to forget how to work
- took the preacher to Martin's Store in E-town for a new suit
- didn't wax or polish cars
- hugged Mother at noontime

- never protested or feared growing older
- watched with us the coming of thunderstorms
- didn't want to be fussed over
- thought you might live to see the second coming of Christ
- rejected the doctrine of eternal security
- believed that the earth was about six-thousand years old, but commented kindly on a fossil collection for geology class
- often began your prayers "Our kind and gracious heavenly Father"
- said during your illness, with the assurance of someone who had purchased his ticket a long time ago, "I guess I'm headed for the Great Northwest."

Contents

Preface

This book is about old gifts. Not about glass canes, tintypes, frakturs, wedding dresses, and shaving mugs. But ten old things, nonetheless. Gaiety, Purity, Civility, Dignity, Simplicity, Generosity, Perceptivity, Responsibility, Serenity, and Integrity.

Books about such things don't just spring up. I know where this one comes from. Actually, it wasn't from Bill Bennett (*Virtues*)[1] or Stephen Covey (*Principle-Centered Leadership*).[2] Both contribute significantly to recent discussions about moral judgment.

The origins of this book are more personal. A year ago, three important things were happening at the same time. Dad was dying; our college was celebrating its centennial; and my upper-level communication class was pondering culture and values.

As I watched my dad finish his days, I was inspired to think of the principles he lived and died by. *Values.* As the college retold its story, I was energized by the strength of men and women in its history. *Values.* As students reported their research on the making of contemporary popular culture, I was stimulated to seek for fixed points of vantage from which we could see our world critically, creatively, and compassionately. *Values*. The topic of old values was common to all three events.

As the year ushered me through a process of grieving, celebrating, and thinking, I sensed that I was unwrapping, as for the first time, boxes of wonderful gifts —gifts handed down.

Gifts handed down has a double meaning. The gifts come down from above, graces from the Divine Source of all bounty. The gifts also come down through the ages, eventually to my dad, to be given to me to give to my children, who have already begun wrapping them for *their* children.

These ten gifts, valued through the ages, provide a measure of character. But you'll be relieved to know that this book is not a set of preachments. In fact, I've worried a bit about sounding like a prude, wagging a finger "naughty, naughty." Anyone observant and compassionate enough to know the eternal tussle between ideal goal and real circumstance can't be a prude.

I do not want to be a negative old man taking out his end-of-life anxieties on a younger generation that seems to be having a lot of fun. I don't see these gifts being enhanced by sanctimony or by sanctions. They're gifts, the kind you enjoy looking at, the kind you like to open, the kind you are most grateful somebody thought to give you.

One afternoon while working on these essays along Lake Michigan, two curious swimmers stopped to ask what I was writing. One was a high-school counselor, the other a psychologist. I spoke in generalities, but they persisted, so I told them the title and chapter topics. "Hmmm," said the counselor. "Where I work, we no longer have those . . . did you call them gifts?" As they moved down the shore, I wondered about our world and our time. Are these gifts passé?

Today there may be more emphasis on credentials than on character. To get ahead, you try to get another degree, or at least add an interesting line to your résumé. But credentials and character aren't the same thing. I've been teaching long enough to know that a student's earning an A in a course is not a measure of virtue.

During Farmers Week at Little Eden Camp on Portage Lake, near Onekama, Michigan, I presented these chapters as little speeches. I am grateful for that attentive audience (Grabers, Kandels, Freys, Lefevers, Weidelichs, and others) and their encouragement. Grace Whitehead was the first to suggest they be published. The campers gave many helpful comments. So many afterwords, in fact, that I asked one of the participants to write an Afterword to the book. She is Rita Kandel Smith, a librarian at the University of Florida.

Long before Bennett and Covey and other contemporaries thought about the topics of this book, the apostle Paul wrote a memorable line to which I'll bracket some additions (Gal. 5:22-23).

> *By contrast, the fruit of the spirit is*
> *love* [instead of hate],
> *joy* [instead of sadness],
> *peace* [instead of stress],
> *patience* [instead of panic],

> *kindness* [instead of incivility],
> *generosity* [instead of selfishness],
> *faithfulness* [instead of infidelity],
> *gentleness* [instead of crudeness],
> *and self-control* [instead of intemperance].

There is no law against such things.

I particularly like those final words. No law against them! They are gifts for which one never needs be ashamed. Let's proceed to open the first gift—Gaiety.

—*J. Daniel Hess*

"cheerfulness . . . festive or joyous activity"

Gaiety

The first gift is a merry heart.

Imagine, but not for long, a planet filled with long-faced grumps whose chief occupation is finding fault. From the infant's first cry until the dying person's final breath, all you'd hear is complaining. And worse, whining. Get me a one-way ticket out, fast.

What we have is happily different, thanks to God, who set the example. On the very first day of Creation, the Lord sat back and said something like, "It just doesn't get any better than this! It's GOOD."

Gaiety. An artist at work. Children tumbling down the embankment at Grandma's house. The wonderful agony of sisters trying to eat lunch, but instead doubled in laughter. A reader, sitting by the June lilacs, turning the page of the latest novel from her favorite writer.

The highly contagious cheer of the neighbor who calls the shots from his front-porch chair. The delight of a story told by the campfire. A saint, in prayer, feeling the shiver of ecstasy in having again been touched by the divine.

Sometimes in jokes, other times in effervescent pleasantness, and many times just in private and simple appreciations where a universe of pleasure is distilled into exquisite joy—gaiety is a gift most treasured.

Solomon says (Prov. 17:22),

> A cheerful heart is a good medicine,
>   but a downcast spirit dries up the bones.

Drying Up the Bones

In the best of all possible worlds, people enjoy good cheer. Unfortunately, the catalogue of reasons for a downcast spirit comes in several volumes.

Surely there are understandable circumstances for a downcast spirit. Physical and emotional suffering can be a heavy burden to carry. Depression can turn day to night, whether it's brought on by chemical imbalance, the wear and tear of stress, or habits of negative living.

No one hopes for genuine disappointments, and yet life offers them in abundance. Disappointments, if catered to, can inflate themselves into general gloom and doom. But the ultimate disappointments are the ones to avoid. If a person has to ask, "Is that all there is to life?" disillusionment attaches itself to cynicism. Snarls seldom hide the hurt inside.

Another cause of heaviness is evil. When one must cover for one's own wickedness, says Solomon, "even in laughter the heart is sad" (Prov. 14:13).

To be sure, one can't be smiling all the time. As they say, life isn't a bed of roses. We sing the blues when things go bad, but wonderfully creative people have even turned the blues into soul-satisfying art. A cloudy day, for some people, is a dreary day. Others look at the clouds for what they are and rejoice.

And then, what shall be said of sanctified cheerlessness? We can follow goodness and mercy all the days of our life and never bless a soul. Our earnestness —on behalf of our preferences, our preoccupations, and even our religion—can actually be a deterrent to meaningful relationships. Earnest spontaneity is an oxymoron.

Misery, they say, loves company. There's long-faced Morose slouched beside Sullen. What a pair! Another such couple is Woe and Waste. It's much better not to attend their parties.

But enough of the problems. Let's be joyful!

The Faces of Gaiety

Gaiety won't stop, sit down, and allow itself to be analyzed. Nor does gaiety want to perform before passive spectators. And dubbed-in laugh tracks are anathema to gaiety.

Gaiety is people having fun. Grandpa's almost inaudible chuckle. Aunt Laura—bless her heart—with her raucous guffaw. John's total-workout chortle. Ruth's cackle that shakes the building.

When meeting some people, you're soon in good spirits just because you're near them. The winsome personality of Miss Wert, second-grade teacher. Miss Kaylor, opening the seventh-grade windows as wide as they go, then pounding the piano and yelling her happy way through the songbook. Mr. Berger's teasing jokes. Mr. Frey's droll sense of humor.

There are people so skilled in communicating their humor that they can make a living as comics: Dave Barry is off the wall, and I enjoy him. And "Car Talk!" Who would have thought that two mechanics could talk about cars and their crazy drivers, and laugh loud enough to be heard across the nation? Yes, and "Far Side."

Gaiety can be loud and boisterous. A town at its summer fair, the youth group in a water battle at the beach, grads slinging their caps into the air.

On the other hand, gaiety can be a quiet, deeply satisfying experience. Farmers bringing in the last load of corn in October, a hiker in a tropical rain forest, a co-ed reading her mail.

Which brings up the subject of words. Words win the good-humor contest hands down. Try to name them, and you won't get finished. The banter of a locker room. An evening of Scrabble. Conversation with witty people. Storytelling. Jokes.

Nevertheless, some good-spirited people don't need words. They are and just keep on being delightful—period. Their near environment, everything within eight feet of them, is tilted toward light.

To Each His Own

Comedians are in high demand; I am no comedian. Clowns are funny; actually, I'm not funny. But there's no need to cry about not being heir to every skill of humor. Most of us have been granted quite enough to fill a life with merriment. Let's be grateful for good times.

I had to think of my fate in grade school when children regularly talked about the Saturday matinees. Or television. Seemingly every day, they rehearsed Milton Berle. I had no idea what was going on; I couldn't laugh at any of it. My family didn't go to movies, nor did we have television, so I missed out. But on the farm, life was good. We had so much fun that the town kids loved to come for a visit.

Just as there's no need to complain about a circumscribed range of gaiety, so there's little profit in belittling another's sense of humor. What they have may be one of their most prized and fragile possessions. Think of infants who experience the cooing and funny faces of their parents in the first year of life. But it's downhill from there. Think of youth who in their teen years never share happy times with their parents. Think of married couples with nothing to say to each other. We do well to encourage the faintest ember of joy.

Let's share our gaiety by telling each other about our good times. Garrison Keillor was probably the most famous person who ever ate at our table and slept in our house. Once he was asked to identify a moment so good that if it were possible, he would want to be transported to that moment and enjoy it all over again. Keillor paused in thought. "Well, ten o'clock this morning was pretty good!"

What have been your moments? As we show and tell, gaiety gains momentum. As you compile your list, I'll take writer's privilege to share a couple of mine, both as a way for me to repeat the pleasure and as a way to stimulate your recall.

It. Remember how much fun we had being it? Sometimes we volunteered, sometimes we went through the process of "One potato, two potato, three potato, four" to find the one to be it. Many of our games needed an it: tin-can alley and t-y-turkey, for example.

Outhouse humor. We all had outdoor toilets, and outhouse jokes abounded. Our joke was in real life. Everybody in the community knew that our outhouse blew over. Ha, ha, ha! But the local lumber store wouldn't sell boards to build a new one. All its lumber had to go to rebuild a barn destroyed by a fire. (I knew the words *spontaneous combustion* before they were added to the dictionary.) A cow barn had priority over a toilet (*priority* is another word I'll never forget). Again, ha, ha, ha! Jake Snyder said he had an extra two-seater. The men moved that one. Its roof had blue shingles, so we thought it far better than the one that blew down.

Childhood play. The corn barn served best for alley over, especially at dusk. One team would throw the sponge rubber ball over the roof. Anyone on the other team who caught it would sneak around and try to hit and thus capture a member of the other team. The corn barn had two advantages: it was high, and it had little barn banks on each side to trip escapees.

Music. My lifelong pleasure in choral music began long ago. At the breakfast table, we sang a cappella through the hymnal. Mother sang soprano, Erma took the alto line, I was tenor, and Merv bass. Dad could sing any of them, so he helped where needed.

Birthing. We rigged a little platform onto the back

of the Farmall BN and headed out into the meadow in the early morning. By the woods we found Betsy and her calf. We petted Betsy to reassure her, then carefully lifted her calf onto the platform. Betsy followed close behind as we slowly drove back to the barn.

Family reunions. When the Abram Good family met for a reunion in Spring City, there was no somber church service and no boring reports. Instead, we had a cheery meal, then a ball game. But apparently Uncle Samuel hadn't played ball. He was told where to stand and how to swing. Uncle Samuel was big. He whacked the first ball beyond the outfielders and stood there watching it go. "Run, run," yelled his teammates. Confused, Uncle Samuel headed toward the pitcher. "No," we yelled. "To first base." He headed for third. It was a stand-up triple. All of us laughed so hard we knew we'd be back the next year.

Playing at work. Making hay was hard work. Barley was dirty, but hay was heavy. And hot, in the field, lifting bales onto the wagon when the thermometer rose to 90. We turned the job into fun by trying to stack the perfect load. This meant placing bales exactly straight, then crossing bales to tie them together so the load wouldn't shift. The biggest challenge was to finish out so we had a perfectly boxed load. From the ground, we couldn't throw an eighty-pound bale to the top of five layers on the wagon. So as we neared the finish, we'd hoist bales, layer by layer, to the top of the load so they could later be dropped into the final places. Then we'd ride triumphantly to the barn.

Pranks. One November first, the morning after Halloween, we awoke to find our barn and sheds emptied of equipment. We found them all bunched together, facing the far corner of the meadow. How did the pranksters keep Lassie from barking?

Rainy days. When the weather was hot and dry and the potato crop seemed to be failing, we prayed for rain. When finally it rained, we celebrated by cleaning the garage and sheds. Dad worked side by side with us. Ivan the hired man helped while cutting up.

My buddies. Four of us—Nevin, Harold, Paul, and I—became a quartet. We sang throughout our high-school years at reunions, church services, campgrounds, youth gatherings, fire halls, summer Bible schools, and street meetings. Without a name, we just sang. Sometimes we got an ugly plaster-of-paris ceramic for singing at a wedding.

Ice skating. It was wrong. It was dangerous. But we did it, and it was fun. We college guys, after lights out, threw pebbles against their window. The girls came out, and we went midnight ice-skating on a deep lake. A great night until Paul fell in. Fortunately, he didn't sink completely below the ice. Paul told us to move away from the break, pushed against edge of the ice with his foot, rolled away from the hole, and was safe. We wrapped him in a blanket and continued skating on the other side of the lake.

Christmas Eve. We drove our young family toward Pennsylvania on a cold December night. Snow slowed us down, but on the radio we listened to Handel's *Messiah*. We caught the wonder that the magi must have felt.

An epiphany. Our job surprisingly took us to Costa Rica to lead students in international study and service. One evening, returning from San Isidro with a group of energetic and delightfully naughty students, we topped the cordillera only to behold highest drama. There to our right and low lay the Pacific Ocean. The sun was setting in spectacular color. We were in awe. We stopped the bus, and all of us got out and stood there dumbstruck. How could beauty be that extraordinary? Someone began singing; we all joined in, "O Lord my God! When I in awesome wonder . . ."

The perfect meal. We had gone with our young family to see cave drawings during our sabbatical year in Spain. Afterward, we were hungry. As usual, we parents wondered where in a foreign town we might find a satisfactory restaurant, especially for children. In town we stopped by an eating house-bar. We opened a door. The bar and tables were filled with loud Spanish men. The owner, noticing our hesitant entry, came to the door. In a moment he knew we were foreigners. And we had little children. Ah, this called for special favors. "Thank you, thank you, I shall serve you," he proclaimed. The men made way. A table was set. The owner became our waiter. The local wine, of which he was so proud, was presented. Then the soup. The salad and bread. Next the lamb chops. Flan. And finally coffee. It was a perfect meal.

Word fun. Among our family games was a homemade guess-the-word game. A person would give three or four clues, the rest would guess the word. For example: (1) Four in baseball. (2) A soup needs it. (3) Vulgar. The answer is *base.* Then little Ingrid wanted her turn. (1) A girl. (2) I blank Grandpa and Grandma. (3) What you do to a porch. We were all stumped. Her answer: *miss.* Her older sibs, the newspaper carriers, knew all too well that a porch was to hit or miss.

Outdoor picnic. North of Chicago at Ravinia, we spread the cloth, ate our lunch, watched the stars come out, then joined Peter, Paul, and Mary in a twenty-fifth anniversary concert. We and our adult children re-sang our way through their childhood with the likes of "Puff the Magic Dragon."

Family tradition. On a plane from Minneapolis to Spokane, a stewardess brought the dinner tray to my son. On it was the dried fig that's been passed from one family member to another for lo these many years.

Jokes. But which ones? I happen to like jokes that play on words. Such as this one which I first heard decades ago, and it stuck with me.

> Bill has trouble remembering names. So Jane gives him advice. "Bill, if you want to become a memory whiz, just learn to associate a name with an object. For example, if you meet Mr. Biddle, associate it with fiddle."
>
> Good advice. Bill goes to work on the association game, but then meets a challenge when he is introduced to Mr. Lomach. Lomach? What on earth can he associate that with that? He thinks and thinks. Oh, stomach! "Lomach-stomach, Lomach-stomach," Bill sings to himself as he walks away, confident that he will always be able to name Mr. Lomach.
>
> Weeks pass. A month. And then one day Bill is walking down the street and sees this man approaching him. Who is he? What was the word association he used when he first met him? He furiously reviewed his memory, and then it came. He approached the man confidently. "Good morning, Mr. Kelly."

I am also partial to jokes about me and my profession. For example:

> Once there was a college professor who dreamed that
> he was in class giving a lecture. It was a long dream.
> When he got awake, sure enough, he *was* giving a lecture.

"Of all the gifts bestowed by nature on human beings, hearty laughter must be close to the top," says Norman Cousins.[1] In the midst of a life-threatening illness, he discovered anew what Solomon said way back there. But, adds Cousins, "Laughter is just a metaphor for the entire range of the positive emotions. Hope, faith, love, will to live, cheerfulness, humor, creativity, playfulness, confidence, great expectations—all these, I believe, [have] therapeutic value."

We've enjoyed one gift. Let's move on to another.

"impurities besmirch, weaken, and distract"

Purity

One summer day Dad and I were cleaning the barn floor, making room for the harvest of new barley. I was young, less than ten. As I swept the floor, Dad as usual was quiet. How I wished he'd talk more with me! About anything. I continued pushing the broom until the thought came to me: I myself might get a conversation started. I could do it with an interesting question. And then a question formed itself, a puzzle that included an intriguing word I'd just heard on the playground from the Dennis boys.

"Daddy, where'd all this *confounded* dirt come from?"

He looked at me with a start, came over abruptly, and smacked me across the face. "To teach you clean talk!" he explained.

I was more shocked than bruised. *Confounded* was a dirty word? I didn't know that. Later I secretly consulted a dictionary and still couldn't quite see the filth, but I knew it must be there somewhere.

As days and years passed, enough in fact that Dad and I could talk about the incident, I was not left with a residue of anger about his impulsive punishment based on meager information. Instead, I gained an appreciation for the strong tradition that gave Dad a regard for language free of slang, free of strange words, free of anything else that damaged good style.

Dad grew up in a day when a boy's "dirty mouth" was forcefully washed out with soap. He lived by a rule that out of the mouth should come blessing, not cursing (James 3:10).

I never heard my father swear. Well, I admit that when he pinched his finger hooking the wagon to the Farmall, I once heard him say, "Oh, sugartit!" That's as close to godless talk as I ever heard from him. Harry "give 'em hell" Truman had little honor with him.

My dad never told dirty jokes. He never made a racial or ethnic slur. When he became angry, he bit his tongue and walked away, for better or worse. His attitude toward language was not unique to him. His community and the community before him avoided foul language.

To understand this seemingly puritan attitude about language, one must recognize that it was part and parcel of a conviction about purity in general. "Blessed are the pure in heart: for they shall see God" (Matt. 5:8, KJV). This beatitude from the Sermon on the Mount was frequently quoted in our circles.

Purity—having to do with all of life, from language and sexual behavior to thoughts and dreams—purity was a grace to fervently pray for, with the words of Mrs. A. L. Davison:

Purer in heart, O God, help me to be;
May I devote my life wholly to Thee.
Watch Thou my wayward feet,
Guide me with counsel sweet;
Purer in heart, help me to be.

Purity: Dated and Quaint

It seems a long linguistic and moral path stretching from that barn talk with my father to contemporary street talk. Lingo today encourages candor and explicitness. Talkers like to surprise and even shock. Easy speech, making a habit of four-letter words, seems to specialize in vocabulary from a lexicon of human orifices and excrement. I admit to being shocked when a student tells me she's "pissed off" about something.

When "naughty" words first found their way into radio or TV programs, they were bleeped out. Today it's probably a tough job to be the bleeper—how does one know when to bleep? The word bleeped yesterday is in today's headline.

Language purists complain that our culture has been too permissive with language. The school of language analysis called normative linguistics emphasizes the correctness and oughtness of language. Another approach, descriptive linguistics, studies "language as it is used." And language-as-it-is-used is changing rapidly, thanks to technological and electronic innovations, rapid communication, and access of minority and regional speakers to public discourse. Even the school curriculum encourages language making rather than language guarding.

We have lost a communally regarded purity of language, such as one finds established and enforced by dictionaries in the King James English tradition. This parallels a deeper trend in twentieth-century moral philosophy that discredits so-called universal standards of correctness.

Moral pluralism has been welcomed. Media, especially MTV, movies, and commercials, have taken voice and picture to the outer margins of culture. Pauline Kael, the film critic of *The New Yorker*, wrote, "I lost it at the movies." She could use the words to indicate not only a personal loss of innocence at the theater, but also a cultural shift in the arts from a commonly enforced code of behavior to moral pluralism.

So we may conclude that purity is a somewhat quaint yardstick for measuring speech. It seems to belong to the old days. If purity is mentioned in public, it has to do with ingredients of soap or the relative quality of heroin. Perhaps the most obvious purity these days is the hygienic routine in some hospital wards.

Back to Basics

The traditional sense of purity as Dad used it is understood by its opposite—impurity. *Impurity* suggests lack of cleanliness, lack of uniform quality, and unwanted additives. Impurities besmirch, weaken, and distract.

When a child walks in mud, the new white sneakers lose the value they had when they were neatly wrapped and smelled of fresh leather. In this case, mud is the impurity.

When a barn is painted with a red that has too

much yellow in the paint, it's not barn-red paint. When iron ore is dug, it has to be smelted to get rid of unwanted nonferrous elements. When buying rock salt, one reads the label to see how clean it is. In these cases, unwanted ingredients are considered impurities.

Similarly, when a married person has voluntary sexual intercourse with a partner other than his lawful spouse, he adulterates himself, or makes himself "inferior by adding extraneous or improper ingredients." [4] The additive, in this case, is an impurity.

When I as a child used the adjective *confounded,* my utterance, in the view of my father, wasn't cursing but was ordinary talk damaged by an additive.

Although purity seems dated and quaint, I want to recommend it as a treasured gift handed down, a grace that can bless us in this day.

Voices of Purity

The God of the Hebrews was held up as the model of refined purity: "The words of the Lord are pure words: as silver tried in a furnace of earth, purified seven times" (Ps. 12:6, KJV).

Purification, both as a religious rite and a code of daily behavior, held central place in the Hebrew tradition. Children were taught the difference between clean and unclean foods. Adults were instructed on the nuances of clean relationships. Priests carefully followed instructions on how to purify the temple.

In the early Christian era, purity was elevated into a doctrine of spirit. Early Christians said that the blood of Jesus, God's Son, cleanses people from sin (1 John

1:7). James, an apostle of Jesus Christ, wrote of practical holiness and often refers to purity in his epistle. "Religion that is pure and undefiled before God, the Father, is this: to care for orphans and widows in their distress, and to keep oneself unstained by the world." "Cleanse your hands, you sinners, and purify your hearts, you double-minded" (James 1:27; 4:8).

Since the early Christian era, our tradition of faith has not ceased to honor purity. This metaphor of cleansing found its way into our hymnals. "Wash me, O Lamb of God, wash me from sin" (H. B. Beegle). "Wash me, and I shall be whiter than snow" (James Nicholson).

Thomas Merton, the beloved Trappist monk from the Gethsemani monastery in Kentucky, wrote, "Humanly speaking, our efforts to show our love for God by purifying our hearts, refresh and delight Him. It is for this that He 'thirsts.' His *sitis* [desire] is for the purity of our hearts, the emptiness of our hearts, that His joy, His freedom, and His immensity may fill them." [5]

In addition to these voices for purity from our religious heritage, I hear and read comments about purity from seemingly nonreligious contexts, from people taking a second look at the morality of current culture.

Joan Gould, author of *Spirals: A Woman's Journey Through Family Life*, writes in *The New York Times Magazine* about sexual purity. She regrets that virginity has declined as a social value among both males and females. Chastity as a component in family values is a matter for scoffing. She comments about people who think that "virginity is considered a failure of courage, . . . a form of immaturity that has to be discarded."

Gould claims that virginity is a "source of feminine strength" that grows in a "Secret Garden, lush but un-cultivated, where each woman sits alone, a garden that might look like a desert to some women and a prison to others, but [is] always a place of silence amid the noise of the city, surrounded by a wall that [has] only one door. " She decries that "the Secret Garden has been converted into a tenting ground." [6]

A Joan Gould-type voice should articulate this same message for males.

Stephen R. Covey, the author of *The Seven Habits of Highly Effective People*, writes:

> Just as the education of nerve and sinew is vital to the athlete and education of the mind is vital to the scholar, education of the conscience is vital to primary great-ness. Training the conscience, however, requires even more discipline. It requires honest living, reading inspiring literature, and thinking noble thoughts. Just as junk food and lack of exercise can ruin an athlete's condition, things that are obscene, crude, or porno-graphic can breed an inner darkness that numbs our highest sensibilities and substitutes the social con-science of "Will I be found out?" for the natural conscience of "What is right and wrong?"
>
> People with primary greatness have a sense of stew-ardship about everything in life, including their time, talents, money, possessions, relationships, family, and even their bodies. They recognize the need to use all their resources for positive purposes, and they expect to be held accountable.[7]

Indeed, there are voices that articulate the rele-vance of purity in our time. Can we expect purity to be not only an ideal but also a practice at home and in our ordinary business? That is to say, can the old-fashioned virtue of purity maintain a crucial place in the contemporary world?

Notes on Purity

Occasionally my own desk wears a note card with a reminder of things greater than the day's agenda. Here is a series of notes about purity.

- Purity may seem old-fashioned. It is—very, very old. And enduring.
- The ultimate source of purity is the pure mind of the eternal God.
- Life gives us many choices; we are to commit the mind to purity, to direct thoughts to noble ideas.
- The pure heart is nourished in solitude.
- A person with a pure mind and heart never need worry about who will find out.
- Impurities besmirch, weaken, and distract. When lusts dominate, a victim should confess them. When additives cling, a host should get rid of them.
- If you pray for cleansing, know that this refining process may be arduous.
- If from the mouth comes blessing and not cursing, then into the person must go honorable nourishment.
- One's near environment—attire, decor, sounds, activities—all bespeak a measure of personal purity.
- The reward for living a pure life is not public recognition but private serenity.

My father would not have minded my comment about the dirt on the barn floor, but he thought it unnecessary to call it *confounded* dirt. In these essays, I honor him and his parents and grandparents for handing down an uncompromising regard for pure, unadulterated living.

"decency . . . public politeness"

Civility

The checker at the food market cracks her gum. The driver gives a crude finger gesture. The secretary interrupts a conversation to answer the phone—these are signs of the social disease of incivility.

Today you can find a meanness of spirit among soccer fans, neo-Nazi youth gangs, and politicians. Radio talk-show hosts raise their ratings by being rude.

Incivility moves like an infection from the car radio to the parking lot to the office. "What d'ya want?" snaps the clerk to the customer. "Put it over there" is the gruff instruction to the delivery agent. Instead of saying a gracious greeting, the seller grabs for the credit card.

Should old-fashioned civility be declared an endangered species?

What Is Civility?

By civility, I mean decency. Public politeness. According to Richard J. Mouw, author of *Uncommon Decency*,[8] civility is "tact, moderation, refinement and good manners toward people who are different from us."

Being civil to each other is the opposite of being boorish, loutish, or uncouth. Here is what I mean.

> I'm working hard as the host in a busy restaurant. It's an August afternoon with a temperature in the 90s, the tourists are tired, and their children are thirsty. But the waiting line at the restaurant is told it will be thirty minutes. The people inside the air-conditioned restaurant know a good thing when they feel it, so they settle back for slow recuperation by ordering big meals-with-dessert.
>
> Outside, the promised wait of thirty minutes turns to sixty, then seventy, then eighty minutes. I don't want to chase away the insiders who are sipping from their coffee cups ten minutes after they finish peanut-butter pie, but I know the people outside are well beyond their limit of patience.
>
> I try to hold things together. Then a desperate call comes from the receptionist. According to her, one man who's been waiting in line for an hour is irate. Could I offer help? I step outside into tension. I try to make explanations, but no apology on my part helps. His voice and fist raised, he tells me up which orifice I should shove the business. I prepare a retort, but I see the receptionist throw a warning finger over her lips.
>
> At this moment as I look at the unlovely, unlovable, crude, crusty, and sweating overweight man, I wonder how to find the personal resources to be civil, to have what Ernest Hemingway called "grace under pressure."

The story is not hypothetical. I really did work in a restaurant, a self-imposed summer "internship" where

I had opportunity to observe and practice public manners. There I encountered people of both extremes—those who had left their etiquette at home or lost it along the way to worldly pleasures, and others whose spirit was unendingly thoughtful, patient, and generous.

The contrast between civil and uncivil people has led me to understand better what constitutes civility. Being civil is far more than being nice. It has to do with one's elementary bearing toward self and toward the other, even when the other person is unlikable. A civil person conveys a dignity that reflects both an inner serenity and an outer regard for the human race. "Love your neighbor as yourself," says Jesus (Matt. 19:19).

Civility is not an external show turned on and off by the push of a button. Civility is being. It is based on constancy—here today, here tomorrow. A civil person, alone is his room, is still respectful.

A Communal Resource

While civility finds its source in deep spiritual springs of awe and reverence, it runs its course through all of life in words, emotions, considerations, and courtesies. It is a virtue that contributes to the environment of home, workplace, church, and social gathering.

Manners are a personal matter. However, one must also recognize the communal character of public decency. What Jacques Barzun said of intellect can be said of civility:

Civility is the capitalized and communal form of live etiquette; it is humane consideration stored up and made into habits of discipline, signs and symbols of cordiality, causes of thoughtfulness and spurs to emotion—a shorthand and a wireless by which the mind can skip connectives, recognize decency, and communicate respect. Civility is at once a body of common good and the proprieties through which the right particle of it can be brought to bear quickly on the matter in hand. Civility is community property and can be handed down.[9]

The human family, over centuries of time, has learned that life is more convenient and enjoyable when people are civil to each other.

Losing a Sense of Decency

But if civility is a communal resource, a culture can lose its shared sense of decency. Our emphasis on individualism has gradually led us away from being group-oriented to being self-centered. As we are devoted to our own success, committed to our own well-being, preoccupied with our own needs, concerned with our personal rights—we become indifferent to public manners.

A culture that is product-oriented rather than person-oriented is likely to put less time and energy into investments of gracious human interchange.

Some of us notice a shift, especially in the United States but also in Canada, away from recognized standards in speech, attire, and behavior, almost to an abhorrence of formalities and a rejection of authority.

Newsweek, in a cover story recently, featured the trend toward "dressing down." Friday informality is in. Jeans are in. Even while we enjoy the benefits of relaxed rules, we wonder if some people read informality as license for incivility.

Many of our communities have dropped the use of titles and roles in addressing each other. Nieces and nephews rarely use the titles of uncle and aunt. However, in traditional Indonesian families, younger brothers recognize by title even an older brother. Similarly, China reveres its old people, while many of ours have no meaningful title or name.

When I began teaching in 1964, I was addressed as Doctor or Professor. A decade later I was Mister. In the 1980s, I became Dan, and now occasionally "Hey." Such informality is thought to break down barriers and classes. But perhaps in public manners, it has led to boorishness.

Civility in the Workplace

Institutions, such as churches, schools, factories, or offices develop their unique cultures. Over time and experience, each institution establishes its purpose, its ways of making decisions, its vocabularies. It also establishes and maintains a particular civil character. Some institutions are formal, others are informal; some are rough, others are refined.

An institution's civility can hardly remain hidden, especially in the intersections of commerce where people of highly contrasting cultures meet each other.

How civil is your workplace? When was the last

time you audited your civility? When was the last time
your staff had a meeting to discuss their public manners?

How would you, your colleagues, and outsiders to
your organization answer the following questions?

- Do employees in your workplace pause, look you
  in the eye, and give a greeting?
- Do people remember your name?
- Do the environmental factors of sound, smell, and
  decor contribute to human dignity?
- Are signs and bulletin board items in good taste?
- Is personal space respected and public space made
  comfortable for everyone?
- Do employees treat people courteously, regardless
  of ethnic, racial, gender, and age diversity?
- Are complaints received with tact?
- Is language clean?
- Do people dress with self-respect?
- Do people listen as skillfully as they speak?
- Do employees clean up after themselves at the
  drinking fountain, lounge, or kitchenette?
- Are people who empty the wastebaskets addressed
  by name?
- Do employees gossip or talk behind someone's
  back?
- Does humor put down disadvantaged persons?
- Do people keep their promises?
- Can people discuss differences without losing their
  cool?
- Is candor honored with confidentiality?
- Are employee networks open?

- Are commendations and criticisms handled with equal discretion?
- Are gatherings and leave-takings marked by courteous words?

The answers to these questions might help you set an agenda for in-service training. Civility can be both taught and caught. The leaders of an organization, not just the receptionist, can model the expected level of civility.

You may also find that paying special attention to civility in your workplace will help make you conscious of civility in your church, your neighborhood, and your home.

Cultures and institutions, including your own, that truly value civility find generous ways to reward good manners. For in honoring decent behavior, we foster public politeness. Civility, after all, is community property.

Dignity

I was returning to Chicago from Denver, riding coach in 1960. It was night; passengers slouched into sleep; the coach smelled of sweat. Then the train stopped in Iowa City.

A passenger got on, a tall, erect gentleman, clean-shaved and neatly dressed. He was a traveler whose deliberate selecting of a seat and stowing of suitcase showed his experience in travel. His face conveyed both awareness of passengers and a respectful remove. Most curious to me, he wore a Mennonite plain coat.

I too was a Mennonite but unfamiliar with travel, and even less acquainted with Mennonites who made their way confidently in the world. My Mennonites were more at home among themselves.

As the train pulled out of the station and passengers reshaped themselves into strange letters of sleep, the cultured Mennonite remained poised, calm, as though in meditation. I left my seat; I had to meet him.

He identified himself as Sanford Yoder. Well into our conversation, I learned that he was a teacher and that he had been president of Goshen College in northern Indiana. Later I learned that he was a legend, a former mule driver turned church and education leader. When describing S. C. Yoder, people used the word *dignity*.

Years later, when I taught at Goshen College and attended chapels, I thought of S. C. Yoder when students sang one particular song. It seemed to me that such a hymn must have been his daily prayer.

> Be Thou my vision, O Lord of my heart;
> Naught be all else to me save that Thou art,
> Thou my best thought, by day or by night,
> Waking or sleeping, Thy presence my light.
>
> Be Thou my wisdom, be Thou my true word;
> I ever with Thee, and Thou with me, Lord;
> Thou my great Father, I Thy true son;
> Thou in me dwelling, and I with Thee one.
>
> Be Thou my buckler, my sword for the fight;
> Be Thou my dignity, Thou my delight,
> Thou my soul's shelter, Thou my high tower;
> Raise Thou me heavenward, O power of my power.[10]

Defining Dignity

What privilege is more special than to meet a person of dignity! What task is more difficult than to define dignity!

Dignity is like the Spanish word *duende* (an elf, elusive). In Spain we heard our friends speaking with admiration of someone who had *duende*. "What is *duende*?" we'd ask them. Their eyes would brighten, their hands would be raised to begin making gestures, but words would fail them. They'd reply, "*Duende* is . . . well, it's . . . it's just *duende!*"

To understand dignity, it's easier to go to examples than to words: Marian Anderson, Arthur Ashe, Robert Frost, Mohandas Gandhi, Dag Hammarskjöld, Henry Cabot Lodge, Peter Marshall, Golda Meir, Eleanor Roosevelt, Margaret Chase Smith, Jessica Tandy.

Dignity is a presence. A presentation. The way one chooses to meet the world.

When S. C. Yoder stepped onto the train, he was making a presentation. What caught my eye from the beginning was his coat. That's appropriate, because dignity is a coat. Those who have dignity wear it like a cloak. It is simple, fitting, and altogether appropriate, consistent with all other aspects of the wearer.

The cloak accomplishes opposite effects at the same time. It reveals and it conceals. It reveals character, attitudes, tastes, manners, and disciplines. In contrast, it conceals what is not public property. It protects privacy and preserves what flourishes best in solitude.

In many persons of dignity, one senses a remove, a bordered garden whose careful tending takes time and space. Dignity regards the usefulness of distance. Because of spatial distance, the person of dignity doesn't throw herself at the first comer. Temporal distance allows her to think before talking, to deliberate before acting.

Dignity associates itself with good taste. Usually the person of dignity does not dress or comb in a manner to shock himself or others. Yet it is common to find this same person looking well-dressed in what might seem outlandish on another person. Attention to the coordination of details may be the difference.

Language is most revealing of one's dignity. Unlike the person who gushes, grovels, babbles, and flatters, the person of dignity opts for words "fitly spoken" (Prov. 25:11). Thus there is a grace, precision, and economy in their discourse.

Dignity links arms with integrity. The dignified person has outer qualities such as good grooming, good posture, correct speech, and exemplary behavior. These are faithful expressions of inner refinement.

Indeed, we must be mindful of counterfeit dignity whose outer garment is an unreliable show. Edwin Arlington Robinson (1869-1935) tells us of one such sad case.

> Whenever Richard Cory went down town,
>   We people on the pavement looked at him:
> He was a gentleman from sole to crown,
>   Clean favored and imperially slim.
>
> And he was always quietly arrayed,
>   And he was always human when he talked;
> But still he fluttered pulses when he said,
>   "Good-morning," and he glittered when he walked.
>
> And he was rich—yes, richer than a king—
>   And admirably schooled in every grace;
> In fine, we thought that he was everything
>   To make us wish that we were in his place.

So on we worked, and waited for the light,
  And went without the meat, and cursed the bread;
And Richard Cory, one calm summer night,
  Went home and put a bullet through his head.[11]

Robinson's poem reminds us that externals can sometimes mislead. What glitters is not necessarily gold . . . or dignity.

While true dignity is a presentation to the public, it is more than an appearance. It is more than the cloak. Like good theater, dignity uses costumes but only because costumes help to accomplish its deeper revelations.

Dignity is a manner of appearing that reveals what's inside. One *has* dignity; one *is* dignified. A person of dignity not only *has* poise, but also *is* balanced, stable, and composed because of an inner guidance system. A person of dignity not only *has* control, but *is* a commander of himself, given to disciplines of thought and emotion. A person of dignity doesn't have to orchestrate attention; he quietly claims it.

The Loss of Dignity

To have to put up with a crude person is unpleasant. But to see an otherwise dignified person in the act of losing his or her dignity is to experience tragedy. Dignity is so valued a virtue that its loss makes us want to hide our faces.

An old 1930 film, made by the German director Josef von Sternberg, gives us an idea of the pain of lost dignity. Entitled *Der blaue Engel* (The blue angel), the story features a strict but dignified high school bachelor teacher (Emil Jannings) who, in the act of punishing his boys for attending a naughty vaudeville show, succumbs to the wiles of Lola-Lola (Marlene Dietrich), a member of the traveling troupe. In the ensuing scandal, he loses his job, then leaves town with Lola-Lola.

Months later when the troupe returns to the village, the schoolboys crowd the theater for a glimpse of their former professor. What they see is burlesque, but it isn't funny. Their respectable professor has been turned into a rooster whose attempts at crowing on stage elicit feelings of dreadful horror.

People of virtue do not rejoice in seeing a human being fall. Instead, like a family that protects a member suffering from a debilitating and deforming illness, so compassionate people help each other to guard their dignity.

I was witness to a less-serious faux pas, involving a guest lecturer. Our campus was surprised that such a notable personage would accept an invitation to come for a one-day round of lectures. The college was small, no fair match against state universities, who could give decent honoraria to famous guests. On the day of the visit, the faculty did its best to host the speaker and be worthy of his stature.

However, something curious happened. The guest was to give a special address to the student body. Prior to the event, he went to the restroom and then immediately entered the lecture hall. He had caught his shirt in his fly zipper and didn't know that his shirt showed through the trousers. In this moment of stunned embarrassment, all eyes fixed on his face, not daring to stare lower. The moment—actually it was more than an hour—was a crisis. Dignity, his and ours, was given an unusual test.

There is chapter 11 bankruptcy for someone who loses money. There is no such chapter for someone who loses dignity. Little wonder that the Greeks who saw tragedy on their stage left the theater cleansed. They had experienced and pondered the personal meanings of tragic loss.

Finishing Schools

Part of the vocabulary of the American educational scene is the finishing school that trains girls in social graces for life in polite society. The curriculum is likely to include issues of etiquette and carriage, high manners and cultured correctness. People in other stations of society may scoff at such attempts to polish the facade of immature youth. Yet the concept of completing one's preparation for life in society deserves another hearing in our era.

Talk-show hosts whip guests and audiences with their tongues, basketball players slug each other, preachers beg for money, comedians try to get laughs from the coarseness of buffoonery, hucksters yell at us on TV, and the mood in the office is just plain nasty. In other words, dignity is somewhat difficult to come by.

We can do our souls and those of our youth a splendid service by building a finishing school for developing dignity. What might the curriculum look like? What marks a person of dignity as being finished? Certainly it is something other than power dressing, assertiveness training, rhetorical excellence, proper affiliations, and political correctness.

The most elementary curriculum would have two parts. The first would help learners gain self-respect. Dignity begins in a confirmation of one's own worth. It is sustained by an acceptance of one's limitations and a husbandry of one's thoughts, emotions, and talents.

The second part of the curriculum would help the learner recognize the dignity of others. For a field experience, I recommend working with what Christ calls "one of the least of these" (Matt. 25:40). In validating another person's worth, one comes home to dignity.

Jean Vanier writes,

> The greatest suffering of the mentally handicapped is to feel "different" and "useless." He needs friends who will help him to discover his own personality and his place in society, friends who love him and respect him. But most of all he needs the Love of God which he may discover through them.[12]

A student of mine, whom I'll call Lori, offered a testimonial confirming the truth of Vanier's words. She said that a person of dignity recognizes the dignity of other people. Instead of imposing one's will on others, and thus wrapping up one's dignity with a bow to give as a gift to another, the person of dignity knows the true value of the gift of allowing another person to have dignity, too. To help me understand her point, Lori related an experience from her summer job of working with Miriam, who had multiple sclerosis.

> I arrived as Miriam was finishing breakfast.
> "Would . . . you put . . . the applesauce . . . in the

frig?" she asked me. Of course. The jar was family-sized and heavy. After it was stored, I noticed the smaller container of milk on the table beside Miriam.

"The milk?" I asked her.

"I . . . can do that . . . myself," she said. At that moment I knew what was my gift of the morning to her. A recognition that she did indeed have the will, the strength, and the coordination to do this task.

Dignity begins at home but doesn't remain there. One leaves home dressed in respect for oneself and properly attired to meet one's neighbors. There is much to learn about them, their customs and cultures, their values, their well-being, the limitations they live with, their work, their faces. One is properly attired to meet them, to accept them, and to receive them in their own noble humanity.

It's an unfortunate oversight if we search the offices of the executives and directors for dignity when dignity is most authentically expressed by the person who empties our wastebaskets.

I return to the train in Iowa City. That night I left my seat to meet this gentleman. I was curious to know more about him. Part of the story I have not yet told. He received me kindly and openly, and then proceeded to learn more about me than I did about him. And his inquiry of me was an affirmation I shall never forget.

"a way of life free from much entanglement"

Simplicity

A little book, smaller than most paperbacks, has survived the numerous cullings of our bookshelf. Its title is *The Journal of John Woolman.* Woolman, a Pennsylvania Quaker, wrote it sometime between 1743 and 1748.[13] Here is a passage that I underlined years ago.

> My mind, through the power of truth, was in a good degree weaned from the desire of outward greatness, and I was learning to be content with real conveniences, that were not costly, so that a way of life free from much entanglement appeared best for me, though the income might be small. I had several offers of business that appeared profitable, but I did not see my way clear to accept any of them, believing they would be attended with more outward care and cumber than was required of me to engage in.
>
> I saw that a humble man, with the blessing of the Lord, might live on a little, and that where the heart was set on greatness, success in business did not satisfy the craving; but that commonly with an increase of wealth the desire of wealth increased. There was a care on my mind so to pass my time that nothing might hinder me

from the most steady attention to the voice of the true
Shepherd.

Woolman's words "care and cumber" have been
for me a continuing wind through the trees, a breath of
the Spirit, telling a secret unknown in this part of the
world in these latter years of the twentieth century.

I wish I could meet Woolman today. Perhaps he
would invite me to his cabin. He would hang my coat
on a wooden peg. Instead of ushering me into a plush
living room with a state-of-the-art entertainment center, he'd offer to me a bench where we would sit and
listen to each other. Later he would provide a lunch of
bread, cheese, and an apple.

I'd be especially interested in talking with him
about business, how he keeps things simple. I'd like to
hear more about what he thinks contributes to "care
and cumber." And surely I'd ask whether his daily
prayer and meditation as well as journaling and attending Quaker meeting affected his business success.

Perhaps we'd talk of an earlier model of simplicity,
one who lived from 1182 to 1226. I can hear Woolman
telling the story: Francesco di Pietro de Bernardone,
son of a cloth merchant, was energized by "a general
spirit of worldliness."[14] Later, after suffering from im-
prisonment during a war and ill health, he experienced a vision of Christ and heard a call to a life of service.

He renounced material goods and family ties and
embraced a life of poverty. As a priest he "composed a
simple rule of life" to imitate the life of Christ. We
know him today as Francis of Assisi, the simple priest

who fed the birds. He founded the Franciscans and
gave us this prayer.

> Lord, make me an instrument of Thy peace,
>> Where there is hatred, let me sow love;
>> Where there is injury, pardon:
>> Where there is doubt, faith
>> Where there is despair, hope;
>> Where there is darkness, light;
>> Where there is sadness, joy.
> O Divine Master, grant that I may not so much seek
>> To be consoled, as to console;
>> To be understood, as to understand;
>> To be loved, as to love.
> For it is in giving that we receive;
> It is in pardoning that we are pardoned;   ·
> It is in dying that we are born to eternal life.

Francis of Assisi, a Catholic, and John Woolman, a
Quaker, are of a kind. Both in their times were conscientious objectors to care and cumber. Their lives of
simple devotion contrast sharply with the care and
cumber of our contemporary scene. How shall we describe it?

> We answer the phone a lot and make many calls.
> We work long hours to get stuff done.
> We have many bills to pay, many people to contact.
> We carry schedule calendars with us.
> We put on a lot of miles.
> We want our business to grow.
> We do things fast.
> There's too much paperwork to do.
> We stay at work too late; we come home tired.

Worldwide web. Cheap airfares. Fresh seafood in midwest restaurants. Global equity funds. Six-lane interstates through the heart of urban congestion. Mars explorations. CD ROM of the River Nile. SportsChannel. But I admit that in the midst of postmodern cacophony, I hear calls for a simple life.

My ambivalence about complexity and simplicity is emphasized because I grew up in an Amish-Mennonite community at a time when my people still thought of themselves as "the quiet in the land." The Amish bishops warned that rubber tires would take people to the world, and that telephones would bring the world to the people.

I watched the Amish farmer make a quality of life from a thirty-five-acre farm, a quality that later five-thousand-acre farm factories couldn't produce. I grew up in a Mennonite family that worked and played and ate and prayed together. Radio and TV came later. Our Mennonite plainness was a comfortable companion to simplicity. Care and cumber were held to a minimum.

But what does that heritage mean if your profession calls for a Ph.D., a United Airlines frequent-flyer credit card, and Windows 95?

Keeping with Simple Company

Is it possible to live the simple life in complex culture? Some people may try to answer this question with a yes or a no. I can't. To live a simple life is a goal for me, not a dogma.

To help me toward this goal, I try to keep company, in person and through books, with people who value simplicity, those who don't capitulate to the "sound and the fury" of legion voices. Such people are available if one looks for them.

My friends who model the simple life shall be given the privilege of their privacy. But I shall report on ten people who make good company for me through their writings. When life gets complex, I turn to their words.

Ernest Boyer spoke with a soft voice, quiet adjectives, and understated gestures. One wouldn't suspect that he held many honorary degrees, had been chancellor of the State Universities of New York (SUNY), U.S. Commissioner of Education, and president of the Carnegie Foundation for the Advancement of Teaching. His list of honors was long. Education was his passion—college education, high-school education, and with a recent publication, elementary education.[15]

Boyer constantly dealt with the turmoil of our school systems. Yet at the heart of his message was a concern for basics, for renewing our sense of top priorities, and for holding to central principles and values as we invest in our children.

Eliot Coleman, author of *The New Organic Grower*, has argued that "you can make a good living on five acres or less of intensive vegetable production. . . . You must watch out for the trap of more, more, and more."[16] Paul Hawken says of Coleman, "Simply stated, I know of no other person (what shall we call him—field gardener, truck farmer?) who can produce better results on the land with an economy of effort and means. He has transformed gardening from a task, to a craft, and finally to what Stewart Brand would call 'local science.' "[17]

Annie Dillard writes about large and small things, near and far. "She is a fine wayfarer," says the *New York Times Book Review*, "one who travels light, reflective, and alert to the shrines and holy places." In *Pilgrim at Tinker Creek*,[18] she can look down into the water at dusk and see distant galaxies racing toward their destinies. Says Buckminster Fuller, "She archingly transcends all other writers of our day in all the simple, intimate, and beautiful ways of the natural master."

Doris Janzen Longacre responded to a commission to elicit information from families on lifestyle, particularly food habits. "We are looking for ways to live more simply and joyfully, ways that grow out of our tradition but take their shape from living faith and the demands of our hungry world." The result is the widely used *More-with-Less Cookbook*, which inspired other more-with-less projects.[19]

Thomas Merton, a Trappist monk who above all else wanted to give his life to contemplation of God, was called by his supervisors to write. Beginning with *The Seven Storey Mountain*,[20] his many books have inspired readers the world over to a love of God. "The eyes of the saint make all beauty holy, and the hands of the saint consecrate everything they touch to the glory of God," he wrote. "When we are one with God's love, we own all things in Him."[21]

Anna Quindlen resigned recently from writing an op-ed column for *The New York Times* in order to write novels. In 1992 she received the Pulitzer Prize for Commentary, largely for her column "Public and Private" in which she discussed the impact of public issues on individual citizens. To read her was to gain a new understanding of the significance of current events. A recent book of hers is *Thinking Out Loud.*[22]

Satyajit Ray never won a regular Academy Award, but in 1992 the academy presented him with a Special Lifetime Achievement Award. Among his best-known films are the Apu Trilogy, composed of *Pather Panchali, Aparajito,* and *The World of Apu.* Ray depicts ordinary life in the Bengal region of India, but his simple style speaks universal eloquence.

Ryne Sandberg is included in this list as a representative of the many skilled professionals who make a difficult job look easy. Considered by many to be the best second baseman of his generation, he received the National League Gold Glove for second base every year from 1983 to 1991. He was National League most valuable player in 1984 and National League home-run leader in 1990, and played for the National League All-Stars from 1984 to 1993.

Whether the Cubs won or lost, it was a memorable day at Wrigley Field, just to watch Sandberg's elegance as a batter and fielder. Never, not even when his error-less play extended over several seasons, did he call attention to himself. Then, to the surprise of everyone, he "retired" in midseason of 1994 because he was dissatisfied with his level of play. In doing so, he gave up nearly $16 million in guaranteed salary. As this book goes to press, Sandberg is planning to return to baseball. I trust that his character as well as his play will not disappoint us.

E. F. Schumacher is author of *Small Is Beautiful: Economics As If People Mattered.* Prior to writing his significant book, he was a Rhodes scholar in economics, an economic adviser to the British Control Commission in postwar Germany, and the top economist and head of planning at the British Coal Board. But paradoxically, he was also president of an organic-farming organization, a student of Gandhi, and involved in many international organizations that addressed local and small-scale economic situations.

Schumacher opposed what he called the "idolatry of giantism" and argued that "economically, our wrong living consists primarily in systematically cultivating greed and envy and thus building up a vast array of totally unwarrantable wants."[23] We must learn to think, he said, "in terms of an articulated structure that can cope with a multiplicity of small-scale units."[24]

Pete Seeger was born in New York City but gave a powerful but simple voice to Southern folk music. He sang alone, he sang with groups (such as the Weavers), he sang in summer camps, he sang in more than thirty-five countries. Seeger wrote music that spoke against war, racism, poverty, and pollution. We all know "Where Have All the Flowers Gone," "If I Had a Hammer," "Kisses Sweeter Than Wine," and "Turn, Turn, Turn." He encouraged others to make their own music. Although he was unfairly blacklisted from singing for many years for the networks, night clubs, and theater, he has not become bitter.

These are good company. When work days become too long and the issues too complex, I turn to them in the evening for conversation.

The Sabbath Prescription

The institution of the Sabbath rest, presented in sacred Scriptures as a divine command, has helped generations of people to remain sane and healthy. Our foreparents discovered that continual work led, not only to physical fatigue, but also to a loss of spiritual perspective. A Sabbath rest has a way of breaking the relentless pace of work. For generations, rest has been a simple solution to escalated complexity.

Today a Sabbath rest can help us to restore a measure of simplicity to our lives. I know it sounds weird because for many people Sunday is the busiest, nosiest, and most tiring day of the week. Perhaps we need to recreate the Sabbath convention, trying out forms of rest that fit the circumstances of our lives.

For some people, Monday is a better day for a Sabbath than Sunday. Perhaps a daily Sabbath—an hour of rest after six hours of diligent work—would do one a big favor. Give a selected thirty minutes each day to meditation. Find a quiet place away from interruptions. Clear the mind of the office IN box. Allow it to explore new thoughts.

Meet regularly with a group through which you can experience connectedness with God. For many people, this means church. For some, house fellowships. For others, weekly gatherings of committed friends. Whether your meetings be given to recreation, eating, worship, conversation, singing, or simple service projects, discover together what it means to be "sane and simple."

Take a quarterly quiet retreat at a state park, a church or convent, even a motel. Leave at home your wristwatch, cellular phone, and TV set. Carry a simple packed lunch and this prayer by John Greenleaf Whittier (1872).

> Dear Lord and Father of mankind,
> Forgive our foolish ways;
> Reclothe us in our rightful mind,
> In purer lives Thy service find,
> In deeper reverence, praise.
>
> O Sabbath rest by Galilee,
> O calm of hills above,
> Where Jesus knelt to share with Thee
> The silence of eternity,
> Interpreted by love!
>
> Drop Thy still dews of quietness,
> Till all our strivings cease;
> Take from our souls the strain and stress,
> And let our ordered lives confess
> The beauty of Thy peace.[25]

Be different this year—during one of your weeks of vacation, go alone to the desert. The desert for you might be Cumberland Island off the coast of Georgia, a summer campground in northern Michigan, a blustery January week in a Chicago service center, or a brief residence in a college dormitory that sits close to a library.

John Woolman, the Pennsylvania Quaker, said, "A way of life free from much entanglement appeared best for me." His words are an elegant gift handed down, ready for us to unwrap.

"a matter of abundant living"

Generosity

A small plaque hanging in a campus recital hall quietly identifies the donor—a local business entrepreneur. He's widely known and respected for creating a successful company that is the undisputed leader in its field in our region. He's also an unusual man.

One of my students, an adult who returned to campus to complete a degree, told a story about this entrepreneur's generosity. A younger couple from the community decided to start a business of the same kind, located within sight of the established company. The entrepreneur, instead of plotting to conquer the competitor, invited the newcomers to his office, encouraged them in their venture, offered some suggestions, and made available his own resources. Both companies thrived; the two families became lasting friends.

Why didn't the original entrepreneur defend his turf? Why didn't he opt to become a fierce competitor? Why did he favor generosity instead of stinginess?

However one may try to answer the questions, it seems obvious that the entrepreneur's actions speak more of character than of money.

The nature and location of generosity sometimes surprise us. A local pastor tells of a recently deceased ninety-year-old parishioner. Edna had been one of the liveliest yet probably the poorest member of his congregation. She gave freely of her slight abundance. The pastor said he sometimes hesitated to tell from the pulpit of a financial need because Edna would always accept such requests as her personal opportunity, offering a few nickels, sometimes a dozen cookies, to help meet the need. She even requested a one-week loan of a dollar from the church office in order to give alms.

If you decide to look, you'll find generous people near you, some quite rich financially and some obviously poor. They have in common a liberal spirit and a living heart. Stories of their generosity warm us and reveal secrets about how the created world functions best. They give public witness to what makes communities thrive. Such tales sparkle with the joy of living.

In celebration of the spirit of giving, we enjoy hearing again and again Dickens' *A Christmas Carol.* When Scrooge, the miserable miser, gets a new vision of people and of things, we ourselves tingle with joy. Finally Scrooge is saved from spiritual death.

Among our favorite Bible stories is the one about Mary, who took "a pound of costly perfume made of pure nard," anointed the feet of Jesus, and wiped his feet with her hair. Critics later said the ointment could have been sold for three hundred denarii, nearly a year's wages for a laborer. When finished with her generous act, she was not the poorer (John 12:1-8).

"God loves a cheerful giver," and so do we (2 Cor. 9:7).

Where Does Generosity Come From?

One big reason we are moved by stories of generosity is that the truly generous spirit is somewhat rare. Millions of people in North America have never heard the neighbor offer to loan his pickup truck, have never received a surprise cherry pie from the woman down the street, have never been given an afternoon of companionship and conversation with a friend, have not been greeted each morning by a friend's welcoming smile. Those who live in a generous, sharing community are richly blessed.

What builds generosity? Is one person more naturally inclined than the next to give the shirt off his back? In other words, is one born to be generous?

More likely, habits of generosity are learned. I saw my mother preparing plates of food for the post-Depression wanderers. I heard my father telling us to leave our work and rush to the neighbor to help him bring in his hay bales before the thunderstorm broke. I saw fifty men gather to clean up the debris the morning after Kreider's chicken house collapsed. I knew that neighbor Nissley cut thistles out of his wheat so the seeds wouldn't blow onto our field.

I examined tables laden with Christmas bundles that our congregation was sending overseas through the church's relief agency. I knew that farmers, who offered work to German prisoners of war in the 1940s, slipped goodies into their lunch bags. I heard, time and again on the market route, "Make sure the measure is full and running over" (based on Luke 6:38).

Generous parents and teachers help a child move through the stage of calling everything "mine." But an individual's development of generosity is affected by many other aspects of social ambiance. A member of a generous church is likely to contribute liberally to the church budget. An employee of a company that enthusiastically and publicly supports United Way is likely to make a larger pledge than if her company grudgingly participates.

Similarly, penny-pinching is learned. The frightening memories of childhood poverty can tightly close an eighty-year-old's purse. A child who grows up in a closed, ethnocentric ghetto is more likely to distrust strangers.

Influences on Generosity

Generosity seems to be influenced by some strange circumstances. A director of development for a nonprofit organization says that people of certain well-paid professions tend to be tight-fisted. Perhaps charitable giving is influenced by one's choice of career. If you're in one of those professions, you may be acculturated into the profession's traditional spirit.

An individual's generosity might also be a function of her country's attitude about giving. For example, the United States became a model of generosity immediately following World War II, when it embarked on the Marshall Plan to rebuild war-ravaged Europe. Today as the U.S. Congress struggles with the national deficit, many political accountants and ordinary citizens think the government should reduce its current foreign-aid budget. The United States does not feel so generous these days. The country's changing policies of giving may well affect how we citizens handle our own purse strings.

Another factor affecting generosity may be demographics. The rapidly increasing population will have at its disposal fewer resources such as fossil fuels, pure drinking water, prime forests, certain minerals, and possibly food supplies. People will scramble to make a living. In such circumstances, it won't be easy to share hard-earned supplies from one's life-support system.

Economic-class differences are widening. Will the model of the future resemble the current situation in Zaire, where one finds an impoverished nation led by one of the wealthiest people in the world? Trends seem to point that way. In the United States, 40 percent of the wealth of the nation is in the hands of only 5 percent of the people. Class struggle does not bode well for a generous sharing of one's possessions.

These various forces—professional, political, and economic—push and shove at the feeding table. But there may be other so-called internal problems, troubles from within the house of generosity. We see trouble both in the donor sector and in the receiver sector. There are 575,000 not-for-profit institutions in the United States, many of which depend on contributions from donors for at least part of their income. According to Geraldine Fabrikant and Shelby White, charitable gifts of more than one million dollars each totaled nearly $975 million in 1993. That same year, gifts from all donors amounted to $126 billion.[26] It sounds good.

These same authors argue, however, that the big

donors "drive tough bargains" on how charities should use their funds. Further, many donors have specific intentions that their largesse will return them a benefit of some kind.

A friend of mine, fundraiser for an environmental center, says that he no longer believes that there is such a thing as generosity as such. "People don't just give. They give in order to get something in return. If I hope to coax money from someone, I must first show what that donation will give back to the donor." As I'll comment later, I don't think this is entirely bad.

The institution of giving is threatened, at the same time, by the receiving sector. In a nation of giving, charitable organizations that receive our donations can be self-serving as they try to manipulate us. Even individuals on the dole can become manipulative.

Can generosity survive in the best sense of the tradition? In a world of haves and have-nots, of 23 million refugees, of impoverished ethnic and racial groups, can generosity be a thriving virtue?

Generosity Re-visioned

Generosity should be understood as more than a selfless giving of one's material goods to other people. True generosity has to do with a dynamic far more fundamental than that.

Deepak Chopra, a physician who combines Eastern wisdom and Western science in his quest to understand what he calls "the spiritual laws," points out that the universe operates through dynamic exchange, with giving and taking in a harmonious interaction of elements and forces. If the exchange is stopped, there is stagnation and suffocation.

> Giving engenders receiving, and receiving engenders giving. What goes up must come down; what goes out must come back. In reality, receiving is the same thing as giving, because giving and receiving are different aspects of the flow of energy in the universe.[27]

In true generosity the spirit breathes, taking in and giving out. The generous soul communes with the source of life. The giving and the taking then can't help but impact one's relationship with nature and with neighbors. True generosity is a particular condition of being. It expresses itself in the sharing of affection, in the offering of one's person, time, place, or possession. What is crucial to generosity is not whether a person is financially rich or poor, but whether his spirit is at home in community. He who guards his savings can never save enough to be secure. She who gives out of the fullness of her cup will always have a cup running over.

> The more you give, the more you will receive, because you will keep the abundance of the universe circulating in your life. In fact, anything that is of value in life only multiplies when it is given. That which doesn't multiply through giving is neither worth giving nor worth receiving. If, through the act of giving, you feel you have lost something, then the gift is not truly given and will not cause increase. If you give grudgingly, there is no energy behind that giving.[28]

Some Generous Tips

- Consider making Chopra's commitment: "Wherever I go, and whoever I encounter, I will bring them a gift. The gift may be a compliment, a flower, or a prayer. Today, I will give something to everyone I come into contact with, and so I will begin the process of circulating joy, wealth, and affluence in my life and in the lives of others."[29]

- Recover the Hebrew regard for giving the tithe. That's typically known as 10 percent. What is not as commonly understood is that the tenth may apply to income, time, energy, space, and intangibles.

- Learn the pleasure of firstfruits giving. Give away the first strawberry from the patch, the first pup of the litter, the first poem of the week of writing.

- Create an enterprise of giving. A dear friend of mine tends amaryllis bulbs for the sole purpose of giving them away in the months of January and February. She offers to take back the bulb after it flowers so it can be readied for the next year.

- Join generous people who don't go dutch. Their habits of giving and receiving will gradually become yours, since we are shaped by the company we keep.

- Stop giving which makes you feel as though you lost something in the act of giving. Start giving that which multiplies in the giving.

- Purchase some tools or supplies with friends (bicycle, garden composter, paintings) so you can move away from an orientation of "mine" to a community of "ours."

- Be what Stephen R. Covey calls an "abundance

manager" by having "a bone-deep belief that there are enough natural and human resources to realize my dream and that my success does not necessarily mean failure for others, just as their success does not preclude my own."[30]

- Become a volunteer. Your church secretary will be pleased to receive your offer of help. Your county has many organizations that depend upon volunteer support, ranging from childcare centers to retirement homes. I notice how proudly the local hospital "blue coats" wear their name badges.
- Learn to accept gifts with simple, honest, and abundant gratitude.

Generosity is not a matter of law, nor of ethics. It is a matter of character, of being, of abundant living.

"vision turned into good judgment"

Perceptivity

Here's a gift most unusual. It's not handed down with loud ceremony. In fact, the gift isn't always recognized until years or perhaps generations later.

I'm talking about wisdom as it's expressed in good judgment, about intelligence and knowledge, about insight, understanding, and discretion.

Where does perceptivity fit in? I gently argue that it's at the beginning of things. Your vision is the starting point; your good judgment is the end result. A perceptive person is observant, sensitive, aware, knowledgeable, insightful, understanding, discerning, and responsive. In contrast, an unperceptive person at best goes along with the "accepted wisdom," but at worst is dull, stumbling somewhat blindly, missing important cues, and overlooking crucial distinctions necessary for good decisions.

Who Has Wisdom?

Let's imagine that we are seated in a fine parlor in an elegant old castle. An open stairway is before us.

We whisper excitedly in anticipation of a special guest who will descend the staircase to give a speech. There she comes. Her name is Wisdom.

> O simple ones, learn prudence;
>> acquire intelligence, you who lack it.
> Hear, for I will speak noble things,
>> and from my lips will come what is right. . . .
> I, wisdom, live with prudence,
>> and I attain knowledge and discretion.
> The fear of the Lord is hatred of evil.
> Pride and arrogance and the way of evil
>> and perverted speech I hate.
> I have good advice and sound wisdom;
>> I have insight, I have strength.
> By me kings reign,
>> and rulers decree what is just;
> By me rulers rule,
>> and nobles, all who govern rightly.
> I love those who love me,
>> and those who seek me diligently find me.
> Riches and honor are with me,
>> enduring wealth and prosperity.
> My fruit is better than gold, even fine gold,
>> and my yield than choice silver.
> I walk in the way of righteousness,
>> along the paths of justice,
> endowing with wealth those who love me,
>> and filling their treasuries. (Prov. 8:5-6, 12-21)

Then Wisdom leaves quietly, declining to hold a press conference. We mind our manners, leaving the castle as ladies and gentlemen. However, once we have been escorted outside the gate, discussion quickly breaks out. "What did she say? What did she mean?"

One listener recalls that she told us to acquire intelligence and to attain knowledge. Another remembers her saying that she lives with prudence and walks in paths of righteousness and justice. And she gave us a clue about her four pet peeves—pride, arrogance, the way of evil, and perverted speech. We also recall that in the middle of her speech, she called attention to the "fear of the Lord." Her closing remarks all seemed to relate in one way or another to the rewards of diligently seeking her.

The discussion by the gates refreshes our memories, but we eventually leave for home, knowing we'll have to continue thinking about the speech and living what it defines. One question that I carry from the event is this: "Who among us is wise?"

If we knew the answer, we could be followers and learners. We have some general notions of who is intelligent and has good judgment, but the test of time often changes the perspective on such things. What is considered wise in one era is scorned in another.

For example, when the accepted wisdom held that the earth was flat, a person who spoke eloquently of the flat earth could probably charge a fee for his "wisdom." Then along came some people who saw the earth differently. Wisdom was stood on its head.

At one time the accepted wisdom held that bloodletting was a therapeutic measure. How many bloodletting physicians were considered wise then, but later not wise! Yet now some physicians are again using leeches to suck old blood out of wounds.

At one time the accepted wisdom held that only

males could compete in athletic events. Females didn't have the strength, coordination, and spirit. Then some people thought otherwise and proved their point.

In a classic work *The Structure of Scientific Revolutions,*[31] Thomas S. Kuhn identifies pivotal works in the history of science:

- Aristotle's *Physica*
- Ptolemy's *Almagest*
- Newton's *Principia* and *Opticks*
- Franklin's *Electricity*
- Lavoisier's *Chemistry*
- Lyell's *Geology*

All these works, he says, violated the "normal science" or accepted theory of the day. Each of the authors called into question a way of thinking, a paradigm. Such theoretical frameworks include processes of information gathering, procedures of analysis, statements of findings, and eventually conclusions and commitments that fit comfortably into a historical or geographical or philosophic moment.

Each scientist had a vision of scientific theory that challenged the old pattern and set the stage for a revolution. The process in the sciences described by Kuhn also applies to other areas of life. Accepted wisdom serves for a time but is superseded by new wisdom.

Kuhn tries to identify origins of the new visions. It's hard to pinpoint because it lies both within and without any particular endeavor such as science. For want of an answer to the origins of vision, I'm using the term *perceptivity* to include the genius and insight that ushers in a new paradigm. Truly a marvelous gift!

Perceptivity in Common Affairs

This essay is not a call for readers to become famous innovators. Fortunately, perceptivity is not the exclusive property of geniuses. Ordinary people have it, too. I'm pleased to illustrate.

In the newspaper today is a front-page report of President Bill Clinton's call for further restrictions on the advertising and distribution of tobacco. Even though medical studies are consistently showing that tobacco is harmful to health, our political resolve to change the tobacco habit lags behind.

I think of my father, just an ordinary farmer, as a pioneer visionary on tobacco. And I'm grateful. In 1947 when I was ten, our family moved from a little house on Colebrook Road to a great big farm of 120 acres. Instead of being a "hired man," my father would "farm on the half," doing the work but giving 50 percent of the profits to the owner.

Dad's enthusiasm for his new station fell quickly, however, when the owner requested twenty acres of tobacco. This was not unreasonable since ours was a tobacco-raising community. Tobacco was the chief cash crop of the county. My uncles raised it, the church people raised it, and even the preacher raised tobacco.

But my father perceived tobacco chewing and smoking to be dirty, smelly, and degrading. He was so sensitive on this subject that he once quit an hourly job requiring him to unload baled tobacco.

For our neighbors and relatives, there was no issue. They perceived no problem. Tobacco raising was comfortably located within the accepted wisdom of their particular paradigm, their worldview.

This story turned out well. Dad suggested that ten acres be put into tobacco, with all those profits going to the owner. His own ten acres would be planted in potatoes. When the steamer came to sterilize the tobacco beds, the farm's owner saw that my father's heart was not in the work. So to my father's great relief, the owner declared that all twenty acres could be put into potatoes.

Current medical knowledge shows that Dad made a good judgment. But at the time it wasn't easy. I recall hearing other farmers tease him about his tobacco-less farm.

New Perceptions

Today we also exist within paradigms. Our accepted wisdom finds its comfortable fit in contemporary thought structures. While we honor accepted wisdom, I hear Wisdom calling for us to be prudent. Some of our accepted wisdom will remain, some of it will be challenged. May the perceptive people among us recognize and exercise their gifts!

Three topics must be looked at with new eyes. In my opinion these three are burdened with accepted wisdom that unfortunately accommodates faulty assumptions, faulty data, and faulty conclusions. I will state them as simple questions.

1. How can we be better informed about the world?
2. How can we better cultivate aesthetic taste?
3. How can we better discern what is holy?

In discussing the questions, I will try to suggest that old views are giving us outdated pictures.

1. *How can we be better informed about the world?* In a village, both an awareness of and respect for our neighbors help us to be good citizens. We find out what's going on. We help make the place safe and attractive. When there's trouble, we pitch in to help. We help elect the village council. In all of these expressions of citizenship, perceptivity is pivotal.

A person acts on what she is concerned about. What she is concerned about is affected by what she knows. What she knows is in part determined by how she sees, listens, reads, and in a myriad of ways senses the village.

So it is in world citizenship. How we sense the world ultimately shapes our response to it. In the village, we may be in shouting distance of each other. But the outer edges of the world are far away. In villages, news can get distorted. Worldwide, how much greater is the challenge to know what's going on!

Does the TV wake-up show adequately inform you about the world's day? Is the evening news sufficient? Will the local newspaper cover the essential stories? Can you be confident of your knowledge by reading a weekly news magazine?

I have my doubts. Secretary General of the United Nations Boutros Boutros-Ghali recently traveled to Africa. There he "apologized and offered a kind of penance" for the "shame" of the UN and its members for standing aside during the killings in Rwanda.[32] He decried the world's ignorance of their circumstances. "There is a kind of dialectical relation between the attention of a great power and the power of the media," he told reporter Barbara Crossette. "It creates a distortion in our work. What I am trying to do, without great success, is to correct this distortion."

Does world journalism need a new paradigm within which to work, so the typical citizen can know more of the necessary information to respond wisely to contemporary issues?

2. *How can we better cultivate aesthetic taste?* The perceptive person is a connoisseur in our cultural village, paying attention to the productivity of its industry and art, searching for what is good, confirming what is excellent, having the grace to tear down and the imagination to build up, and working with a singular purpose —to enhance the life of the people in the village.[33]

The perceptive person has an old-fashioned, deep, abiding affection for excellence. He searches for "the best knowledge and thought of the time,"[34] hoping to find ideas and art that say YES to life, and to announce abroad, "Behold, it is very good" (cf. Gen. 1:31).

But we're in trouble in our culture making. Even while we make purchases of cultural products, we have increasing disquiet about the aesthetic quality of our ambiance. There is focused concern about violence, power issues, health, family values, and shoddiness in construction.

Perhaps the old categories don't work so well anymore. For example, some people have put art and culture on a hierarchical ladder, as in high culture, middle-brow culture, and low culture. They go on to suggest what kinds of artifacts belong in each category. Perhaps these categories have lost their meaning.

Other observers make a different taxonomy: fine art, folk art, and popular art. As in the previous scheme, adherents put comparative values upon each category, usually elevating fine art and demeaning popular art. But again, one may ask, does this scheme help us to find what is truly worthy of attention?

Current media managers opt for yet another measure in determining what programs and products to produce: what the people will buy. Those programs with low ratings are dropped. Movies that make money seem to stimulate the making of more movies of the same kind. The economic criterion is pervasive.

In what seems to be a retaliation, artists are now making their own private statements in their work, leaving us with artistic chaos. We have come to a point in aesthetic history, especially given our means of production and delivery, to re-vision aesthetic taste.

3. *How can we better discern what is holy?* Moses was tending the sheep of his father-in-law on the side of the mountain Horeb. An angel of God appeared in the form of a bush aflame. Yet the bush wasn't consumed by the fire. Moses stepped closer to see this oddity, only to be stopped by a voice. "Don't come closer, Moses. Take off your sandals, for this is holy ground" (Exod. 3:5, rephrased).

Since history was first written, people have sensed that ordinary things become extraordinary when touched by the divine. People kneel, take off a hat, genuflect, pause in quietness, or pray in the presence of the holy.

And yet, from the beginning of holiness, it hasn't been easy to distinguish clearly what is holy and what is ordinary. Read in Kings the accounts of Elijah and Elisha in their sometimes successful, sometimes unsuccessful attempts to help people around them, even their rulers, to recognize the holy. They built altars, they sacrificed animals, they gave prophecies, and performed miraculous deeds.

The struggle to discern what is holy continues to this day of fortune-tellers, astrologers, and cult leaders. Some New-Age religionists make everything holy, resulting in a sacredness of nothing. Mercenary preachers on TV make a mockery of the pulpit. The religious orders take a regular beating in contemporary TV shows and films.

I detect a trickle-down effect. Kids carry Coke into church. Mealtime prayer seems out of place with fast food. Sunday is the best commercial day of the week for some businesses.

Today's categories of the profane and the sacred aren't very successful delineators of the ordinary and the extraordinary. For too many people, a clerical collar suggests a violation of children, and a sacred place becomes a good spot to establish a trinket shop for tourists.

We need perceptive Elijahs and Elishas for the twenty-first century—people who've been given the special gift of wisdom.

> O simple ones, learn prudence;
> acquire intelligence, you who lack it.
> Hear, for I will speak noble things,
> and from my lips will come what is right.
>
> (Prov. 8.5-6)

"accountability, dependability, doing your duty"

Responsibility

One of the more important tasks as professor is the making (usually writing) of recommendations for students. My files bulge with letters to graduate schools and employers.

I've observed that students and prospective employers differ from each other on what makes promising employability. Students suppose that employers want to know their grade point average (GPA) and their college entrance-exam scores (SAT, for instance).

Students are somewhat surprised when I tell them that in my thirty-two years of teaching and answering inquiries from prospective employers, I've yet to be asked about a person's GPA or whether a student is smart.

It's not that employers don't care about grades and intelligence, but their priorities begin elsewhere. A likely first question from the employer: Is this applicant *responsible?* Students, especially those who haven't been employed, don't get it. I try to explain.

What employers mean by their question may refer to a range of issues—whether you arrive at work on time, show up regularly without absences, look decent, learn a job, and carry out your assignments. Employers differ in some particulars, but they usually have something clearly in mind behind the term *responsibility*.

When I asked my barber for her definition of a responsible employee, she was quick to reply, "Helping out." She explained in more detail. "Let's say one of my stylists is an hour behind. Two others are caught up. They may think their job is done. But no, I don't want them sitting there reading magazines. I expect them to offer to help—a shampoo perhaps, sweeping a floor. I'm talking about teamwork."

The city tennis team captain defines responsibility in different terms. "It's getting a sub if you can't make it, and informing me of the change."

Responsibility, as a dairy farmer describes it, has to do with the way the workers relate to cows! He hires students to help in the milking parlor, a job that consists of moving four cows at a time into parallel stalls, washing the udders, attaching the suction cups, detaching them, and then sending the cows on their way. "This process gets messed up if the worker is flustered. Cows can tell when the worker knows what he's doing. My best employee now is female. She is comfortable around animals and around the machinery. She is responsible."

Responsibility means something else in a customer service office. Employees must be at their desks ready to assist walk-ins and call-ins. The manager explains, "When an employee phones in to say he'll be late from lunch because he needs to research something in the library, I get suspicious. I want him back here fast. "

My favorite definition of responsibility comes from the farming community in which I grew up. I heard this sentence many times: "A good worker stays on the job till the floor is swept."

To be responsible may mean different things in different places, but the importance of responsibility holds steady as a universal virtue. It refers to accountability, dependability, doing your duty, fulfilling your obligations, accepting a task, taking on a burden, completing an assignment satisfactorily.

The responsible person gets up and gets going. She arrives on the job on time. He works diligently when the supervisor is gone. She goes the second mile in helping others. He gets the job done and does it right.

Responsible for What?

The first object of responsibility is yourself. You accept the assignment to care for your health and comfort, taking on what amounts to a moral obligation to be janitor of a human temple. A person who violates his own body or who parasitizes on others is said to shirk responsibilities.

However, responsibility moves beyond the individual; it takes on social dimensions. When a child can care for himself, he is then given additional tasks. As he fulfills these obligations, gaining the reputation of being a dependable person, he is given greater and greater duties.

The ultimate object of responsibility is life itself. We are stewards of our planet and its resources. We are caretakers of all the world's creatures. Its citizens are also our obligation. We guard values. We uphold long-held traditions. We reverence what is holy.

It's readily understood, then, that there's a point to being responsible. It's not just a virtue, but a commitment to serve, conserve, and preserve what is ultimately of value.

Hindrances to Responsibility

Circumstances favor or frustrate one's sense of responsibility. Some circumstances can be eliminated, some can be modified, others must be accommodated.

Physical, emotional, and mental limitations can impose low ceilings on an individual's capabilities. The loss of hearing, the onset of depression, or the damage from an aneurysm—any of these may determine what one can be expected to do.

A bigger problem than physical restriction is the lack of will to be responsible. If a person is marginalized by society, she may feel less motivated to protect that society's treasures. If a person is controlled by a paternalistic system, he may not have opportunity to make the decisions expected of a responsible person. If a person lives in fear of legal retaliation, she may hesitate to take initiatives.

Responsible action relates directly to knowledge, freedom, and conscience. To be responsible is to be informed. Having knowledge, one needs freedom to act on what one knows. Knowledge and freedom need conscience as the rudder. Without the three, responsible action is not likely to occur.

Going to the Dogs?

I suppose that ever since older people worked themselves into habits of reliable behavior, they have bemoaned the irresponsibility of youth. It would not surprise me to learn that in every decade since Adam and Eve's senior years, older people have rubbed their chins and remarked, "Kids these days don't know how to work."

Today is no exception. Many adults, especially school teachers and employers, share their impressions of a rapid fall of responsibility in the younger generation. Employers are complaining these days about unprepared applicants, people not ready to show up regularly, unreliable workers whose productivity doesn't get started until Tuesday and falls off on Friday.

I think I know what they mean, for I too have a continuing disquiet about that minority of students that I'd label as irresponsible. However, the problem seems to turn itself back on us as institutional leaders: we might not be responsible toward our students. At the very time when youth should be learning responsibility, we adults spoil them.

In college, for example, when young bodies are strong and activity levels are high, we indulge the youth. Parents pay the tuition and buy entertainment centers for the dorm rooms and send pocket money. A food service provides the meals, a low-paid worker cleans the toilets, and maintenance erases the blackboards and sweeps the floors after classes. Colleges these days go a step further to arrange weekend entertainment for students. Meanwhile, students are bored, complaining of nothing to do.

It is not surprising to find off-campus student rentals unkempt, student parties loudly offensive late at night, and their attendance at morning classes sporadic.

What a difference I've observed when a college student works his way through school. Jim, for example, was in my organizational communication class which met at eleven. He explained in a class speech his job with UPS. He got up regularly at 3:30 a.m., arrived at work at 5:00, finished his trick by 9:00. He was also carrying a part-time academic load; his work for my class was always done well and on time. Before the end of the semester, UPS had observed his sense of responsibility and offered him both a full-time job and a promotion.

Jim and people similar to him lead me to conclude that if there is an eroding of the foundations of responsibility—on campus, in the workplace, on the highway, in fields and streams—we all have an opportunity to help rebuild these foundations.

The Teaching of Responsibility

The writer of Proverbs gives a wisdom that permissive people might find authoritarian and repressive. But I believe it applies most appropriately to the teaching of responsibility. "Train children in the right way, and when old, they will not stray" (Prov. 22:6).

Responsibility can be taught in a variety of ways such as these: (1) modeling responsibility; (2) identifying responsibility; and (3) telling stories.

Responsibility is taught most effectively by adults who model it. A father who keeps his shop in order provides an example to the child on putting away toys. A family that always arrives at church on time implants an attitude about responsibility into the families. A teenager who helps clear the table and tidy the kitchen sends a message to a younger sibling.

The adult who supervises an apprentice is successful just by showing how it's done. Mother moves in for two weeks to help daughter learn to care for her newborn. It's been done for generations.

In addition to modeling responsibility, the good teacher has to put it into words: This is what is expected of you. Here is what you are responsible for. Words are needed because communities and employers and institutions vary in their expectations. In my neck of the woods, we believe that a responsible person—

- wipes up milk spills
- returns shopping carts to the store
- reads labels on a bottle of orchard spray
- puts tools back where he got them
- informs the neighbor if car lights have been left on
- doesn't let her door touch the car in the next space
- ties a red flag to boards extending beyond a truck bed
- after logging out, stays on if a co-worker needs help
- recycles
- attends PTA and parent-teacher conferences
- gets the car serviced every three thousand miles
- places garbage in containers raccoons can't open
- fastens a seat belt on every trip

- addresses the complaint directly to the party involved
- turns socks right side out, then into the laundry
- leaves a restroom tidy
- returns books to the library on time
- declares all income on tax forms
- flosses his teeth
- on icy mornings leaves home early for work
- replaces the lid on the rubber cement
- gets off welfare or unemployment comp ASAP
- slows down at puddles to avoid spraying pedestrians
- stays on sidewalk instead of cutting across lawns
- tips a good waitress at least 15 percent
- thanks God for food, but helps put it on the table
- cleans up when walking the dog
- reports if the dollar changer sends back five quarters
- trims back trees that touch the neighbor's house
- and makes no excuses.

Usually we assume everyone knows the exact form that responsibility should take. But it's not a bad idea to call the team together—be it family or work crew—and talk explicitly about those expectations.

A third method of teaching responsibility uses stories. The vivid telling of past experience gives us lasting pictures. I think I learned my first lessons about responsibility from the story of Peter and the dike. And about the same time, I was told the story of Noah. His sense of responsibility helped the whole human race to survive.

Another story, encountered much later, comes from Kermit Eby, in "Let Your Yea be Yea." [35] His story of just a few words has given me a continuing picture of conscientious work:

> Grandfather's attitude in regard to work was almost exactly that of Rabbi Joseph, the builder. Both were working ministers responsible for their flock, and both believed that a promise once made placed profound obligations on the maker. The Torah tells of a rabbi [whose] "opinion was once sought on a certain matter, and he was found standing on some scaffolding. The questioner said to him, 'I want to ask you something,' but his answer was. 'I cannot come down because I was hired by the day.' "

All around us, stories about responsibility are being created every day. I want to tell my grandchildren stories from my childhood, of my parents teaching us responsibility. For example, we were supposed to care for the soil. If a rainstorm was washing away topsoil or the wind was blowing it away, we were called to do a better job of protecting it through rotation of crops, windbreaks, contour farming, water channels, and ground covers. The soil, which gave us harvests, was to be fed and left in better condition at the end of the year than at the beginning. We were responsible to preserve the land for future generations.

Recently I saw a woman in a large straw hat bending over the weeds next to the city's welcome sign. On the return trip, I noticed that the weeds were gone, the trash picked up, and flowers were planted by the sign. I met this woman the next day and inquired of her new job with the city. She responded, "I don't work for them. I just noticed the unsightly sign and had the time. So instead of calling to the city manager, I just did it myself."

I opened this essay talking about reference letters. Inquirers are interested in responsibility, I said. To refresh my own memory of their letters, I pulled my file. On top was the most recent one, sent to the University of Washington, from which I quote.

> But academics were not what impressed me most. R_____'s regard for other people contributed to an environment I shall always appreciate. Since R_____ grew up in a home, church, and community that conscientiously teaches nonresistance, his own philosophy of nonviolence is rooted in his own heritage. But he has grown on his own terms, through his reading, through intercultural living (in the People's Republic of China), and through resolving conflicts.
>
> I remember with appreciation his relationships with newspaper staff, his friendship with women, his attitudes toward racism and sexism, his rejection of the exploitative manipulations of mass media, his caring for students whose compositions were not written as well as his, and most immediate of all, his respect for me as a teacher.

A sense of responsibility is a gift to be sought and treasured. For this reason we pray with the Psalmist: "Lord, . . . let your work be manifest to your servants . . . and prosper for us the work of our hands—O prosper the work of our hands" (Ps. 90:1, 16-17).

"inner and outer tranquillity"

Serenity

Out my window to the south, I can see Mr. Sylvester taking down a huge eighty-five-foot maple tree. Mark, our neighbor, was afraid that the dead tree could fall against his house. So he called on a professional tree surgeon.

Mr. Sylvester is in a bucket about fifteen feet from the top or about seventy feet from the ground. (Last week in Nappanee, an eighteen-year-old on a carpenter crew fell to his death from twenty feet.) As I watch the expert, my stomach turns. I should quit watching, but I know that his behavior and the topic of this essay, serenity, are somehow related.

He maneuvers the hydraulic bucket slowly to a site, ties a limb-to-be-cut to another part of the tree. Mr. Sylvester uses a knot that will allow the rope a passage once the limb is cut. Then it can be safely lowered to the ground by a helper below.

I notice how deliberately he works, be it in adjusting the bucket, tying the knot, or sawing. After a cut he examines the tree for the next action, always making sure that each cut will provide for the next anchor and hinge. Before cutting and during the lowering of branches, he keeps vigilance on his co-worker on the ground who is sending small branches through the chopper.

I'm captivated. I pause in my writing to walk through the alley toward the workers. Mr. Sylvester sees me; now I too am a factor in his surveillance. He takes a break, brings down the bucket, and enjoys a glass of lemonade. I compliment him on the neat stack of ten-foot limbs. Then he returns to the skies to continue his work, maintaining thoughtful calmness on the job.

The Age of Anxiety

Mr. Sylvester is unusual. He works with an assurance that comes from personality traits, professional training, and experience. It's inspiring to watch such a worker. In our time, inner or outer tranquillity do not come easily, even in jobs less dangerous than his.

We are an anxious people. Typically we turn to centuries past for examples of dangerous jobs, horrendous plagues, barbarian plundering, and catastrophic disasters. Nevertheless, the age of anxiety is now in our day and place. It does not matter that many workers are covered by health insurance, that the forty-hour workweek provides time for leisure, that salaries give some of us a degree of affluence, and that science goes a long way in making tools safe and in predicting volatile nature. In spite of all that, we are anxious.

People have tight stomachs and sweaty palms because of learned habits of nervous busyness, fear of what could happen, panic brought on by an addiction, depressions from chemical imbalances, too many masters and too many commitments, and desires unfulfilled.

Many are anxious in their relationships, stressed by frictions and diminished by betrayals.

People are anxious because of work and the corporate atmosphere. They know the fluctuating line on the graph of corporate morale. Anxiety comes off the assembly line quickly on those many occasions of legal actions, unfair competition, downsizing, and hostile takeovers.

Mushrooming over all is the threat of violence. People are anxious because nations and groupings war against each other. They do not know when they themselves will be the target of a stone.

Together these many causes have produced our age of anxiety. The spirit is afflicted with a dis-ease that expresses itself in antisocial forms ranging from aggression to paralysis. Our economic prosperity has not lessened this dis-ease. Consumer goods have not served as a remedy.

In this cultural context, then, the words of Jesus are direct and strong.

> Do not worry about your life, what you will eat or what you will drink, or about your body, what you will wear. Is not life more than food, and the body more than clothing?
>
> Look at the birds; they neither sow nor reap nor gather into barns, and yet your heavenly Father feeds them. Are you not of more value than they?

And can any of you by worrying add a single hour to your span of life?

And why do you worry about clothing? Consider the lilies of the field, how they grow; they neither toil nor spin, yet I tell you, even Solomon in all his glory was not clothed like one of these. But if God so clothes the grass of the field, which is alive today and tomorrow is thrown into the oven, will he not much more clothe you —you of little faith?

Therefore do not worry, saying, "What will we eat?" or "What will we drink?" or "What will we wear?" For it is the Gentiles who strive for all these things; and indeed your heavenly Father knows that you need all these things.

But strive first for the kingdom of God and his righteousness, and all these things will be given to you as well. (Matt. 6:25-33)

What Is Serenity?

As Dante illustrated in *The Inferno*, it's easier to make vivid the expression of evil than to describe good. But let's try it. What is known internationally as The Serenity Prayer helps us know the depth and breadth of serenity. It was written by Reinhold Niebuhr in 1943 as part of a service in the Congregational Church of Heath, Massachusetts. A parishioner was moved by the words and asked Niebuhr for a copy, which then was first printed in a monthly bulletin of the Federal Council of Churches.[36] It has come to instruct many of us.

God, give us grace to accept with serenity the things
that cannot be changed, courage to change the things
that should be changed, and the wisdom to distinguish
the one from the other.

Niebuhr's prayer concerns two behaviors, accepting and changing. Both are necessary for serenity, but
the two are different enough for Niebuhr to pray for
wisdom to separate the two.

Serenity as Accepting

The accepting side of serenity has to do with a
present progressive state of spiritual tranquillity sustained by a knowing, a trusting, a relinquishing, a hoping, and a waiting.

Serenity is a *knowing* about proper proportion, the
true size of an issue. This comes from seeing the larger
view, knowing the significance and import of an issue,
and thus grasping the larger purpose.

Serenity is a *trusting* in the plan of God and in the
providence provided by that plan. It is the security of
having universal, complete, and permanent insurance.
Serenity is also a trusting of people, connecting with
them in welcomed interdependence.

Serenity is a *relinquishing* of intemperate desire.
Greed and serenity are impossible allies. Serenity is a
relinquishing of memories that plot ill will, of gossip
that delights in scandal. Serenity is a renouncing of
wars (none of which can be won, anyhow), a surren-
dering of skeletons in the closet, a waiving of the rights
and privileges the caste system has bestowed upon us.

Serenity is a *hoping.* Instead of courting with cynicism that can only mock the model and sneer at the saint, the person of hope is thoroughly convinced of the work of the Redeemer. In that hope, one can begin now to identify with all things bright and beautiful and live with the assurance that the kingdom and the power and the glory will be forever.

Serenity is a *waiting,* a waiting that gives birth to patience. Serenity isn't something that necessarily occurs in the absence of dangers, threats, strife, and stress. Instead, it is a positive condition of knowing, trusting, relinquishing, hoping, and waiting, even in the experience of tumult.

On the other side of the world, I saw one of the most vivid examples of serene acceptance. A film project took a team of us to Site Two, a barbwire-enclosed camp in a desert in eastern Thailand. This was a temporary home for 157 thousand refugees from Cambodia, Vietnam, and Laos.

For people who lived there, Site Two was terror in slow motion. For us outsiders, Site Two was instant shock. One can hardly image the people leaving their countries at night, carrying children on their shoulders, stumbling on land mines, suffering from lack of food and water. Then upon reaching another country, they discovered there was no place to go. Meanwhile, all 157 thousand of them were altogether vulnerable, exposed to vicious enemies, homeless, people with no future.

Prior to the beginning of our filmmaking, we visited camp leaders: the political chair, the hospital administrator, and the head of a women's organization.

While each of those persons was a study of courage and grace, an elderly Buddhist priest made the most-lasting impression. He received us quietly but kindly, even though we came from a foreign country implicated in the regional war. He was comfortable with silence.

Finally the priest spoke softly of the suffering within the camp and of his unending responsibility to help his people to endure. He carried a heavy load of 157-thousand burdens. He looked at us with compassion and thanked us for making a film. He sat in repose. After leaving him, we knew that he hadn't just played a theatrical role of be-calm-for-an-hour but had learned and lived serenity through years of devotion and discipline.

Serenity as Changing

"Give us courage to change the things that should be changed," prayed Niebuhr.

I think of the fierce thunder, lightning, and wind of the storms hitting our farm. In the height of those storms, my parents were calm. They were accepting what they were unable to change, even the loss of a large chicken house. But I observed that there was a prerequisite supporting their acceptance.

My parents got ready for storms. They changed what could be changed—bringing in the cattle, closing the chicken house door, and regularly checking the lightning rods. They prayed and kept house well in their relationships and their spiritual life. They trusted the heavenly Father to work all things out for good.

Recently I read a more contemporary and dramatic example of serenity as change. William J. LeMessurier, a widely respected and prize-winning structural engineer, designed an unusual support system for the fifty-nine-story Citicorp Center in New York City. The building was erected and hundreds of people were at work in it when one day he discovered a series of misunderstandings and miscalculations of the force of "quartering winds." Quartering winds hit the building on a diagonal line, moving against two sides of the building at once. He came to realize that a fierce storm could blow the building over! LeMessurier had good reason to be anxious

This knowledge brought on a dark night of his soul. Should he, a respected engineer, hide the facts and cover his shame? Should he commit suicide? The long night led into morning. Early the next day with exemplary courage, he called together colleagues, consultants, legal advisers, building owners, and even weather advisers. He initiated the Special Engineering Review of Events Nobody Envisioned (SERENE). As soon as possible, they set to work to solve the problem —by welding heavy steel plates over certain bolted joints at a cost of several million dollars.[37] LeMessurier is honored today for changing what could be changed.

Serenity—A Gift Handed Down

When Jesus said, "Do not worry," he did not want us to have to whistle in the dark. Life throws anxiety-producing events our way. But Jesus' call to faith suggests a spiritual state for dealing with forces larger than our strength. They have to do with an elemental condition of being that transcends personality type. That condition then affects how one thinks, feels, and acts.

To live in serenity from Monday through Saturday is to make a daily appropriation of Sunday's benediction, "Go in peace." Sometimes that means waiting in trustful patience; sometimes it means learning how to handle a chain saw safely. And that has to do with who we are as we cut down eighty-five-foot trees, get ready for a tornado, care for refugees, or redesign a building. In peace, in serenity.

"whole, unfractured, uncorrupted"

Integrity

I sing in praise of integrity . . .

honest weights and full bushels
accurate labels and authentic ingredients
fair prices and exact change

the trustworthy news report
the accurate tax record
the performance as advertised

an original lecture
a faithful film
a sturdy house

a natural smile
a warm handshake
a word fitly spoken

a good day's work
sound sleep
a pure dream

I sing in praise of integrity.

Integrity—In Our World?

Ours is a world in which personal integrity is inconvenient, inefficient, and unwieldy. A busy place where procedures can be upset if one bothers with values. A production center where quality control is a function of probability and gullibility.

Words are made to say what they do not mean, a gesture is meant to conceal, action is formed into deception. A small box of cereal is relabeled large. Plastic is grained to look like wood. Pringles are made to crunch like potato chips. Rubber pads are shaped into a size-D breast cup.

In Search of Integrity

To people on the street, integrity has to do with honesty in financial matters. If the bank auditors give a clean bill year after year, decade after decade, its officers come to be known as people of integrity.

Our concept of integrity, when we make of it an accessory or a commodity or a label, may be entirely too small. In *The Journal of Philosophy*, James Gutman has argued that "integrity involves a standard which can supply a possible norm of valuation applicable to our entire system of ethical ideals.[38] In other words, integrity may be the foundation for the whole stone, steel, and lumber of ethics.

An ancestor to the word *integrity* is the word *integer*, used by the Greeks.[39] *Integer* belongs to arithmetic: one, two, three, four, five—any of the whole numbers. In contrast, a fraction is only a portion of an integer.

An integer is whole in that it is a unit, complete and

undivided. A *four* needs nothing more to be a four. A *three* is complete in and of itself; it needs no scaffolding to hold it up. A *six* isn't a lot of pieces.

This ancient ancestor *integer* didn't stand still, however. The arithmetic wholeness and individuality spread to include the larger sense of metaphysical and spiritual condition in people. A *person* could be an integer: whole, unfractured, uncorrupted, distinct, unique.

How might we renew our own esteem for integrity? In our age of strategies, ethics is taken to be less important than success, excellence less important than functionality, and singleness of heart a lesser quality than adaptability and even two-facedness. Barrenness of ideals and alienation lead people to do what is "right in their own eyes" (Judg. 21:25). One wouldn't choose to suffer for the sake of an "ought." In such an age, how might we recover the size and shape of integrity?

Old Models of Integrity

The Greek exploration of the whole, individual human being may be represented by the life of Socrates. He insisted, with the fervor of a radical convert, on doing what he thought. Socrates refused to allow even a crack to fracture thought and action. When the Greek state sentenced him to death for his teachings, he gladly went to his execution. Before drinking the poison his jailer had prepared for him, Socrates urged his friends to desire "a measure of harmonious integrity to our actions and productions, so that . . . our inner and our outer lives may be at one." [40]

Another Greek, Sophocles, produced a play

around 440 B.C. in which a young woman, Antigone, faced a terrible dilemma that tested her integrity.[41] Her brother was killed in battle. Because the lad was involved in a traitorous act at the time of his death, the new King Creon commanded on penalty of death that no one should bury the corpse: "Let his body lie for dogs and birds to make their meal."

Antigone respected her king, but she also knew the claims of a brother's love. She knew the divine law for the Greeks: "to refuse a man burial was the worst of crimes, sentencing him to wander forever a homeless shade, denied entrance to the [other] world." [42]

Antigone did the wonderfully human thing. She made a decision, given these impossible alternatives, to bury her brother and to meet an early death. In the words of Antigone, "It is a noble way to die."

Job's Integrity

The Greeks struggled with the idea of the human being as *integer* and contemplated with awe the terrifying dilemmas of putting human things together and holding them together. Meanwhile, the Hebrews were also pondering the concept of integrity. Not philosophers in the Socratic tradition, the Hebrews nonetheless gave to us an awareness about wholeness that the Greeks didn't know much about.

Where could wholeness be found? Not in people, not in the gods, but in the One. Yahweh alone had power to create the world, to give and to take life, to bless and to curse, to gather and to scatter, to love and to destroy. Yahweh was the eternal, omnipotent, omniscient, omnipresent One, whole and individual, un-equaled. "I am the Lord your God, who brought you out of . . . the house of slavery" (Exod. 20:2).

This was a new idea. Neighbors of the Hebrews—Mesopotamians, Egyptians, and later Greeks—thought the heavens above and the worlds below were popu-lated by bickering and fickle divinities who made mis-chief for earth creatures. Just one god?

For the Greeks, a commitment to integrity in-volved many dilemmas. To the Hebrews, a commit-ment to integrity provided only one decision. "Choose here and now whom you will worship: the gods of your forefathers and of your neighbors, or the Lord" (Josh. 24:15, NEB, adapted).

The Hebrew test of integrity meant a confrontation with God. Yahweh was real and had to be met head-on. What terrible wrestlings took place! Jacob and God. Jeremiah and God. The psalmist and God.

One of the oldest stories in the Bible concerns a man in such a confrontation. Job, whose name is found in texts ranging from the nineteenth to the fourteenth centuries B.C., was an ancient success story. He was a man of "blameless and upright" life, "the greatest of all the people of the east." His earthly status was estab-lished by wealth, servants, a cordial family, and good personal health.

Most important of all, he "feared God and turned away from evil." He had it all together (Job 1:1-5).

Satan argued that Job's goodness was skin-deep. He feared God only because of the kickbacks—social and material benefits. Take away those handouts, Satan predicted, and Job would (1) no longer reverence God and (2) thereby lose the heart of his integrity. It was no small charge.

God accepted Satan's challenge and consented to the grotesque examination: all that Job had was to be taken away—family and possessions and health (1:6—2:6). "So Satan went out from the presence of the Lord, and afflicted loathsome sores on Job from the sole of his foot to the crown of his head. Job took a potsherd with which to scrape himself, and sat among the ashes" (2:7-8).

His physical suffering was compounded by social pressures. His wife said, "Do you still persist in your integrity? Curse God, and die" (2:9). Friends tried to diagnose his problems and to prescribe remedies (2:11; and throughout the book).

Job called for God (7:7-21). God didn't answer.

Job continued to call for God (10:2-21). God continued not to answer. Satan watched.

Whatever the range of Job's temptation, even when everything else was gone, he only called the more for God. Job retained his integrity. The only change wrought by the test was that Job, upon finally hearing from God, revised his own concept of the size of God. God was bigger than he thought; God's purposes were too wonderful for him fully to grasp. His hearsay information about the Lord yielded to more direct experience, a vision of God (42:1-6).

In return, God "restored the fortunes of Job. . . . The Lord blessed the latter days of Job more than his beginning" (42:10-17).

Out of the distant past, both the Greeks and the Hebrews seem to call to us, "Your integrity is too small. Your concept of integrity is malformed. Your ethical vision is eclipsed."

Integrity in Our Time

As we seek to be people of integrity today, let's rediscover several accompanying virtues.

Authenticity. That's what Kermit Eby was thinking about when he commented on "the modesty of character which kept my ancestors from putting the biggest apples or the smoothest potatoes on the top of the basket. Doing so would destroy the discovery of the goodness underneath. Their products, like their lives, were better the deeper they were penetrated."[43]

Veracity. Companion terms are truthfulness and honesty. Frankness and candor. Sincerity. A person of integrity loves the truth to such an extent that the smallest infraction is like betraying a friend, breaking a contract, or turning against a proved guide. "Above all things, do not use oaths, whether 'by heaven' or 'by earth' or by anything else. When you say yes or no, let it be plain 'Yes' or 'No' " (James 5:12, NEB).

Reconciliation. The "big blue marble" earth is marvelously sculpted, carefully trajected in its space journey, and endowed with resources to sustain lives over many years. Yet this planet with human life is in trouble because its inhabitants are estranged from each other, suspicious strangers who live at one address. They want to "cleanse" themselves of strangers.

However, God became incarnate in Jesus Christ, whose sacrificial death can make us one. God has "reconciled us to himself through Christ, and has given us the ministry of reconciliation" (2 Cor. 5:18). This is God's way to restore among us a oneness.

Shalom. Yahweh was the eternal, omnipotent, omniscient, omnipresent One, whole and individual, unequaled. Yahweh intended to give people that same all-encompassing well-being. Just as Yahweh established shalom in the heavens, so the Lord wills wholeness and peace to his people on earth. Thus Yahweh creates integrity!

Henri J. M. Nouwen says that the goal of the Christian is to be a living reminder of Jesus Christ by seeking a life of remembering, healing, sustaining, and guiding. Therein is wholeness, integrity.[44]

Our parents and grandparents tried to take seriously the claims of uncompromised integrity in their day. Can we not do the same in ours?

A Prayer for Integrity

> Lord, you have searched me and known me,
> You know when I sit down and when I rise up;
>   you discern my thoughts from far away.
> You search out my path and my lying down,
>   and are acquainted with all my ways.
> Even before a word is on my tongue,
>   O Lord, you know it completely. . . .
> Examine me, O God, and know my thoughts;
>   test me, and understand my misgivings.
> Watch lest I follow any path that grieves [you];
>   guide me in the ancient ways.
>   (Ps. 139:1-5, NRSV; 139:23-24, NEB)

Afterword

A gift is something someone gives to us, and it generally comes to us without our asking for it. It can be an object, a touch, a place, an emotion, a model for behavior, an attitude toward life, an inspiration. A gift can be new or old. When a gift is old, used, and handed down, its value is often increasing rather than decreasing.

When I turned fifty, a friend gave me a book she had received when she turned fifty, from a friend who had received it when she turned fifty. Part of the joy and value of that gift for me was the list of names and encouragements written on the title page. The fact that it was used enhanced its meaning. I appreciated the gift of the book itself, but the gift of connectedness with other women turning fifty made it very special.

A gift is not given with a restriction on how it should be used. The giver takes pleasure in giving, then lets the gift go. The recipient has the opportunity of using the gift however desired. One takes complete possession of the gift, putting it on display or hiding it in a cupboard, treasuring it or throwing it away.

At the end of a week at Little Eden Camp, Dan asked us to share a special gift we had been given. I didn't have to go far or think long to come up with a special gift I received: it was Little Eden Camp itself. My family began going to Little Eden in the 1950s, and there have been few years since then that we haven't spent a week there in the summer.

As a child, I made friends from other cities and states whom I saw only once a year: Elaine Smucker, from Evanston, Illinois; and Kathy Yoder from Kalona, Iowa. We bought packs of Juicy Fruit gum and would put five sticks in a mouth at once. We bought candy and hid it under our pillows to eat after lights were out. We rode in Smuckers' boat and skied on Portage Lake. We fought the waves and the cold of Lake Michigan and ran barefooted through the dunes.

When we tired of those activities, we walked out to the lighthouse, at the end of the pier. We fished for northern pike. We played Rook and tried our hands at tennis. We read *Little Lulu* comic books and colored in coloring books with brand-new crayons. That was Little Eden's first pleasure for me—being there and enjoying it as a child.

The second pleasure this gift of Little Eden has given me is the opportunity to pass it on, hand it down, to my children. I have seen the pleasure of it renewed in them, the experiences I had there as a child mirrored in their experiences. My children did not grow up in a rural midwestern area as I did. They don't know anyone who farms for a living. They have not grown up in a Mennonite church. Their high school is bigger than the college I attended. But they have gone to Little

Eden for a week almost every summer of their lives.

Little Lulu is gone, and no one buys Juicy Fruit gum from the snack shop anymore. But they do play Rook and buy huge scoops of Mackinaw Island fudge ice cream every night. In the evenings, they sit in the round shelter, laughing and talking with friends from far away that they see only once a year. They try their hand at tennis. They fish and ski on Portage Lake. They swim in Lake Michigan, build sand castles, walk to pier's end, and watch the sunset. They go barefooted. They sing Mennonite hymns with Mennonite singers.

Little Eden Camp is a gift my parents gave me as child, and it is a gift I share with and pass on to my children. It has given me double pleasure, once as a gift received, and once as handed down.

Dan's essays speak of gifts he received from his father. He is handing them down to his children, and now to us, the readers of his book. Dan worries that they have become old. Yet gifts of gaiety, purity, civility, dignity, simplicity, generosity, perceptivity, responsibility, serenity, and integrity become passé only if they are hidden in a cupboard and forgotten.

As recipients of these gifts, we can use them anyway we choose. I encourage you to accept the "old" gifts presented in this book. Take pleasure in them, use them as you wish, as you are able, and then pass them on. Old gifts handed down never become passé. Old gifts handed down are gifts renewed.

—*Rita Kandel Smith, Curator*
The Baldwin Library of Historical Children's Literature
Department of Special Collections, University of Florida

Notes

1. William J. Bennett, *The Book of Virtues: A Treasury of the World's Great Moral Stories* (New York: Simon & Schuster Trade, 1993).

2. Stephen R. Covey, *Principle-Centered Leadership* (New York: Summit Books, Simon & Schuster, 1991).

3. Norman Cousins, *The Healing Heart: Antidotes to Healing and Helplessness* (New York: Norton, 1983), 50.

4. "Purity," *American Heritage Dictionary*, 3d ed.

5. Thomas Merton, *The Sign of Jonas* (San Diego: Harcourt Brace, 1953), 39.

6. Joan Gould, "The Virtues of Virtue," *The New York Times Magazine*, Jan. 27, 1991.

7. Stephen R. Covey, *Principle-Centered Leadership*, 64.

8. Richard J. Mouw, *Uncommon Decency: Christian Civility in an Uncivil World* (Downers Grove, Ill.: InterVarsity Press, 1992), 12.

9. Jacques Barzun, *The House of Intellect* (New York: Harper & Row, 1959), 4.

10. Ancient Irish song, translated by Mary Byrne (1905) and versified by Eleanor Hull (1912), from *The Mennonite Hymnal* (Scottdale, Pa.: Herald Press, and Newton, Kan.: Faith & Life Press, 1969), 300.

11. Edwin Arlington Robinson, *Collected Poems* (New York: Macmillan, 1930), 82.

12. Jean Vanier, *Eruption to Hope* (Mahwah, N.J.: Paulist Press, 1971), 48-49.

13. John Woolman, *The Journal of John Woolman,* ed. and introd. by Thomas S. Kepler (Cleveland and New York: The World Publishing Co., 1954), 20, from chap. 2 (1743-1748).

14. Ignatius Charles Brady, "Saint Francis," *Encyclopaedia Britannica* (1970).

15. Ernest L. Boyer, *The Basic School: A Community for Learning* (Princeton: Carnegie Foundation for the Advancement of Teaching, 1995).

16. Eliot Coleman, *The New Organic Grower* (Chelsea Green, Vt.: 1993), 17.

17. Coleman, xi. Also see Eliot Coleman, *Four-Season Harvest: How to Harvest Fresh, Organic Vegetables from Your Home Garden All Year Long* (Chelsea, Vt.: Chelsea Green, 1992).

18. Annie Dillard, *Pilgrim at Tinker Creek* (New York: Harper & Row, 1974).

19. Doris Janzen Longacre, *More-with-Less Cookbook* (Scottdale, Pa.: Herald Press, 1976), with more than 600,000 copies in print; Longacre, *Living More with Less* (Herald Press, 1980); Delores Histand Friesen, *Study/Action Guide, Living More with Less* (Herald Press, 1981); Linda Hunt, Marianne Frase, and Doris Liebert, *Loaves and Fishes* (Herald Press, 1980), a children's cookbook; Catherine Mumaw and Marilyn Voran, *The Whole Thing* (Herald Press, 1981), a snack-food cookbook; Joetta Handrich Schlabach and recipe editor Kristina Mast Burnett, *Extending the Table* (Herald Press, 1991), with dishes from over 80 countries.

20. Thomas Merton, *The Seven Storey Mountain* (New York: Harcourt Brace, 1948).

21. Thomas Merton, *New Seeds of Contemplation* (New York: New Directions, 1961), 24-25.

22. Anna Quindlen, *Thinking Out Loud: On the Personal, the Political, the Public, and the Private* (New York: Fawcett, 1993).

23. E. F. Schumacher, *Small Is Beautiful: Economics As If People Mattered* (New York: Harper Collins, 1989 reprint ed.), 34.

24. Schumacher, 70.

25. *The Mennonite Hymnal* (1969), 274.

26. Geraldine Fabrikant and Shelby White, "Noblesse Oblige . . . with Strings: The Charity of the Rich Isn't Always What It Seems," *The New York Times*, Apr. 30, 1995, sec. 3:1, 13.

27. Deepak Chopra, "The Law of Giving," in *The Seven Spiritual Laws of Success* (San Rafael, Calif.; Amber-Allen Publishing, 1994), 25-36.

28. Chopra, 29-30.

29. Chopra, 35.

30. Covey, 157.

31. Thomas S. Kuhn, *The Structure of Scientific Revolutions* (Chicago: Univ. of Chicago Press, 1962).

32. Barbara Crossette, "UN Chief Focuses on Africa's 'Underdog Conflicts,' " *The New York Times*, July 23, 1995, sec. 1:3.

33. J. Daniel Hess, *An Invitation to Criticism* (Goshen, Ind.: Pinchpenny Press, 1984), 6-8.

34. Matthew Arnold, *Culture and Anarchy*, ed. J. Dover Wilson (New York: Cambridge University Press, 1969 reprint of 1869 ed.), 70.

35. Kermit Eby, "Let Your Yea Be Yea," *The Christian Century*, Sept. 14, 1955; reprinted in J. Daniel Hess, *Integrity: Let Your Yea Be Yea* (Scottdale, Pa.: Herald Press, 1978), 9-16.

36. John Bartlett, *Familiar Quotations* (Boston: Little, Brown and Co., 1980), 823, no. 15.

37. Joe Morgenstern, "The Fifty-Nine-Story Crisis," *The New Yorker*, May 29, 1995, 45.

38. James Gutman, "Integrity as a Standard of Valuation," *The Journal of Philosophy* 42, no. 17 (Apr. 13, 1945). This article, along with many other resources on the topic of integrity, appears in *Personal Integrity*, ed. William M. Schutte and Erwin R. Steinberg (New York: Norton, 1961), 14.

39. "Integer," "Integrity," *The Oxford English Dictionary* (New York: Clarendon Press, Oxford Univ. Press, 1933). For more detail on *integrity* among the Hebrews, see Hess, *Integrity*, 23-30.

40. Socrates's conversations with his friends immediately before his death are recorded in *Phaedo*. This paraphrase of his words is supplied by Gutman, "Integrity."

41. Sophocles, *Antigone*, trans. and ed. Peter D. Arnott (Englewood Cliffs, N.J.: Appleton-Century-Crofts, Prentice Hall, 1960).

42. Arnott in Sophocles, ix.

43. Eby, "Let Your Yea Be Yea."

44. Henri J. M. Nouwen, *The Living Reminder* (New York: Seabury Press, 1977), 59.

The Author

J. Daniel Hess is the son of Mervin M. Hess and Ella K. Good. His grandparents are John and Mary Hess, and Daniel and Anna Good.

Dan has taught communication at Goshen (Ind.) College for more than thirty years. In 1991 he received the Sears-Roebuck Foundation Teaching Excellence and Campus Leadership Award. Though taking early retirement in 1996, he teaches on a part-time basis and does consulting.

He has published many articles, and his books include *The Whole World Guide to Culture Learning, From the Other's Point of View: Perspectives from North and South of the Rio Grande, Ethics in Business and Labor,* and *Integrity.*

Hess has a Ph.D. from Syracuse University in mass

communication. He has directed thirteen international study-service units in Costa Rica, led orientation seminars for international relief and service agencies, and helped produce a film about refugees: *Journeys of Hope.*

He teaches a course on working in a multicultural world for the Goshen College Organizational Management Program. Since 1967 he has consulted in personal, organizational, and cross-cultural communication.

Dan is married to Joy Glick, and they are members of the College Mennonite Church at Goshen, Indiana. They have one grandchild and four grown children: Courtney Pierre, Gretchen Maria, Ingrid Susan, and Laura Elizabeth.